PRIMITIVE
HOOKED RUGS
for the 21st Century

By Cynthia Smesny Norwood

Copyright © 2015 by
Stackpole Books

Published by
STACKPOLE BOOKS
5067 Ritter Road
Mechanicsburg, PA 17055
www.stackpolebooks.com

www.rughookingmagazine.com

Printed in the U.S.A.

10 9 8 7 6 5 4 3 2 1

On the cover: *Antique Flower Basket*, hooked by Carol Daugherty
Cover design by Caroline M. Stover
Photographs by Larry Norwood, unless otherwise indicated

Library of Congress Cataloging-in-Publication Data

Norwood, Cynthia Smesny.
  Primitive hooked rugs for the 21st century / Cynthia Smesny Norwood. — First edition.
    pages cm
  ISBN 978-1-881982-97-5
1. Rugs, Hooked--Patterns. I. Title.
  TT850.N67 2015
  746.7'4—dc23
                    2014047239

CONTENTS

New England Berry Tree, 30" x 50". Hooked by Crystal Brown of Washington, Pennsylvania. The flowing vine with balls really softens the sharp break from the center design to the outside border. I love the bright leaves scattered throughout the tree. Pattern available from Woolley Fox.

Cynthia Smesny Norwood, a native of Texas, started hooking rugs in 1980. Her first exposure to rug hooking came after she and her husband moved to northeastern Ohio. She saw samples of the craft at the Apple Butter Festival in Burton, Ohio, and she was "hooked." Although she has a BA in history and English, her first love has always been art. Her first hooking projects were #3-cuts—flowers, birds, and Orientals—but that wasn't exactly what she was looking for. Then she discovered a simpler pattern in which she used mainly recycled gray-brown herringbone, with a little peach for color, and hooked it in a wider cut. Like the work of most artists, her work continues to evolve, becoming more primitive.

Cynthia established Star of Texas Rug Camp in Fredericksburg, Texas. She is past director of Cross Creek Rug Camp in Newbury, Ohio, and she founded Winedale Rug Hooking retreat, Round Top, Texas for the University of Texas American Historical Studies Center. She is a past board member and current advertising manager of the Association of Traditional Hooking Artists (ATHA) and a McGown certified teacher. She has exhibited at the Museum of American Decorative Arts and at the Clear Lake Arts Alliance, both in Houston, Texas. Cynthia has participated in *Rug Hooking* magazine's *Celebration of Hand-Hooked Rugs* several times, even serving as a judge. She writes for *Rug Hooking* magazine and ATHA's magazine.

She has taught workshops across the United States and loves seeing everyone's rug come alive. Now semi-retired, she still teaches a few times each year. Contact her at: canorw@aol.com

Antique Garden,
31" x 48". Designer unknown. From the author's collection. Note how some of the originally black fabrics have faded into browns and grays. This rug is composed of various fabrics, not all of them are wool.

When hooking a primitive rug, the rules go out the window! Create your own rug. Keep your mind open, and don't be encumbered by rules and posted guidelines. There are no mistakes . . . remember, this is primitive rug hooking. The women of our past didn't have access to all the wonderful wools we now have, nor did they have time to dye the perfect shade if they ran out of one piece, nor were there tons of suppliers or teachers in the late 1800s or early 1900s. Although patterns were available, frequently the rug hooker simply drew her own design on a piece of burlap. If she ran out of one fabric, she just picked up a piece of any color and finished the area she was working on. All those elements are what makes a primitive rug so fabulous and why we love the old rugs. It's a process that we can duplicate today even though we have the benefit of great wools, dyes, and designers.

Hooking a primitive rug is not just outline and fill—although we frequently do use different or many different wools to outline a design and then use others to fill the design. It is important to first plan how to best fill the design using various textured fabrics to create the desired effect. Color planning is still part of

the process, but we don't mind if part of the design occasionally falls into the background because the value is too close to the value of the background fabric. That look replicates old primitive rugs.

To achieve a good primitive, start with a good pattern—one that is simple, without a lot of detail or fussiness. More importantly, it needs to be one that you really like; one that makes you smile or speaks to your heart. You will give it definition and life by the wools you choose and the way you hook it. If you have a complicated design that you love, simplify it and hook it in a primitive style by removing some elements or enlarging others. You can change any pattern and add whimsy or quirkiness to make it your own.

My hope is that this book will increase your love and understanding of primitive hooked rugs, whether you create them, admire them, or collect them. If you hook rugs, I hope that you catch my enthusiasm and addiction to this style. I can look at a rug I hooked years ago and remember what was happening in my life when that rug was created.

While primitive rugs are part of my life and history, they are also a connection with the past. I hope this book will encourage you to have fun creating *your own* primitive rug!

CHAPTER ONE

Taking an Antique Collection into the 21st Century

Comparison, Adaptation, and Interpretation of Old Primitive Rugs

ORIGINAL RUG **Roses with Leaf Scroll,** 25" x 38". Designer unknown. From the author's collection. The original rug has a medium background that simply echoes the design. Note how the artist hooked lighter fabrics around the corner motifs and the edges of the leaf scroll. I love how the five main leaves are totally different from each other and use various greens. I also appreciate how the pink berries almost fade into the background. You still see them, but they are not sharply defined.

Roses with Leaf Scroll, 25" x 44". Hooked by Debra Inglis of San Augustine, Texas, 2013. Debra used a dark background, which makes the rug more dramatic. While I love the touches of blue, I especially value how she treated the leaf scroll. She made wise use of a lighter background behind the main section of the design.

Samples of fabrics Debra Inglis used in *Roses with Leaf Scroll.*

W hat would happen if you gave line-drawn patterns of old rugs to your friends to hook, but didn't allow them to see the original hooked rugs? What would happen to the patterns from the nineteenth and twentieth centuries as they moved into the twenty first century? Would they be more primitive or less primitive?

Let's start our venture into primitive rug making by taking a close look at a handful of antique rugs and how they can be adapted and interpreted to create modern day primitive rugs.

My new home in Texas has less wall space than my last home in Ohio. So unfortunately, my collection of old rugs spends most of the time rolled up in my wool room. While enjoying them one afternoon, an idea was born. I contacted several rug hookers to ask if they would be willing to participate in an experiment. Surprisingly, they all said yes. The guidelines were simple: hook the rugs with colors you like, use

widths you prefer, make any changes to the design you wish, bind them in any manner, and no, you can't see the original. Furthermore, so I wouldn't influence their interpretation, I did not want to see the rugs until each was completed. I emailed each of them the sketches of the patterns available, and they made their choice. I drew the patterns on linen, shipped them, and assigned deadlines. Then I waited. I hope you find the results as interesting as I did. Several of these rugs are included as free patterns in this book. Due diligence was done in trying to track down the original designers of each pattern.

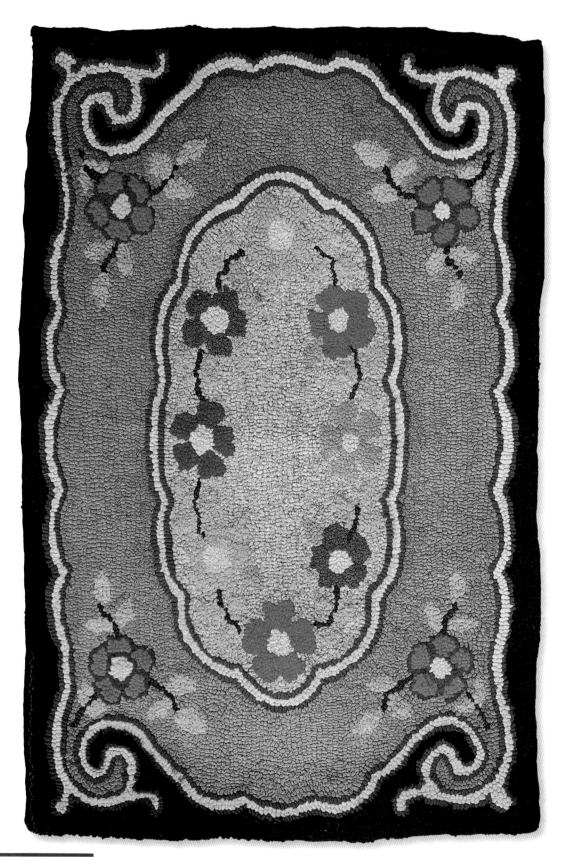

Flowers and Scrolls, 24" x 36". Designer unknown. From the author's collection. The original rug was hooked with yarn as well as wool fabric. The simple design catches the viewer's eye because of the chroma of the colors and their movement. The very dark background keeps it well grounded. You can almost imagine how much fun the original artist had while making it.

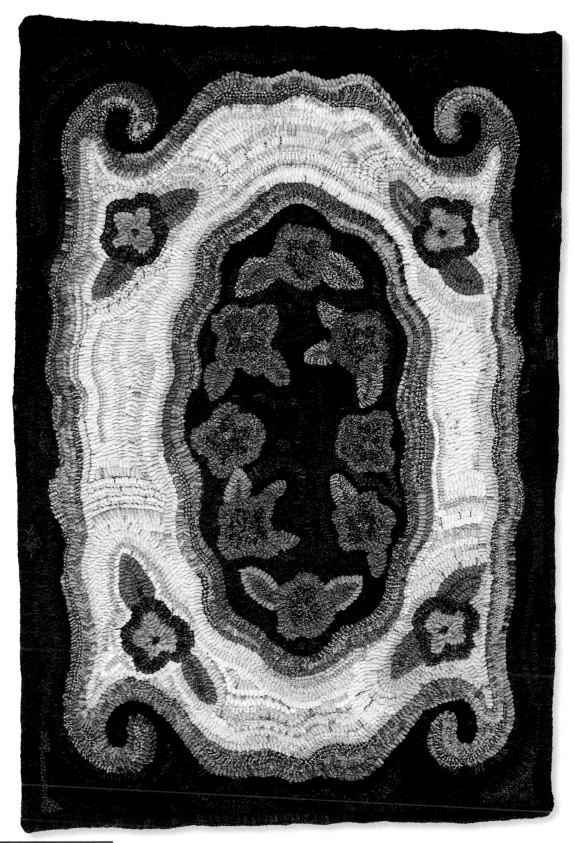

Flowers and Scrolls, 25" x 36". Hooked by Joan Sample of Woodinville, Washington. Joan made a great choice by using a light and a dark fabric for the background then bouncing from dark in the center to light and back to dark again on the outer edge. I love how the scroll creates the medium value in the rug. And those who know me know I definitely approve of the purple in the flowers. Also note the hooking pattern in the lighter background fabric. She showed even more independence by removing the knobs from the original drawing of the scroll.

Three Grand Roses, 26" x 44". Designer unknown. From the author's collection. At first glance this seems like a perfectly hooked rug. But note the two leaves that are outlined with a totally different fabric. You know the rug hooker didn't worry that they didn't match and just kept hooking. I also like how she handled the outer border. It starts and stops on its own, doesn't have straight edges, and doesn't compete with the design. Note how the center background is hooked mainly in straight lines.

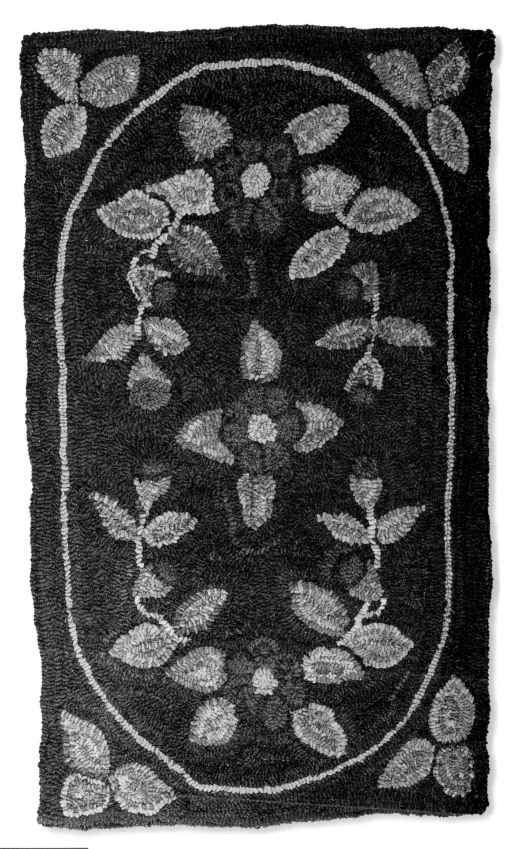

REIMAGINED RUG **Three Grand Roses,** 30" x 50". Hooked by Kaye Swor of Chardon, Ohio. Kaye is a prolific rug hooker who definitely made this pattern her own. She redesigned it to fit her style by simplifying the roses and the leaves. Then she took the design a step further and turned the oval into a beautiful rectangular rug and used the gold line to keep the integrity of the original design. The addition of the corner leaves anchors it perfectly. Note the use of lighter textured fabrics hooked randomly in the background.

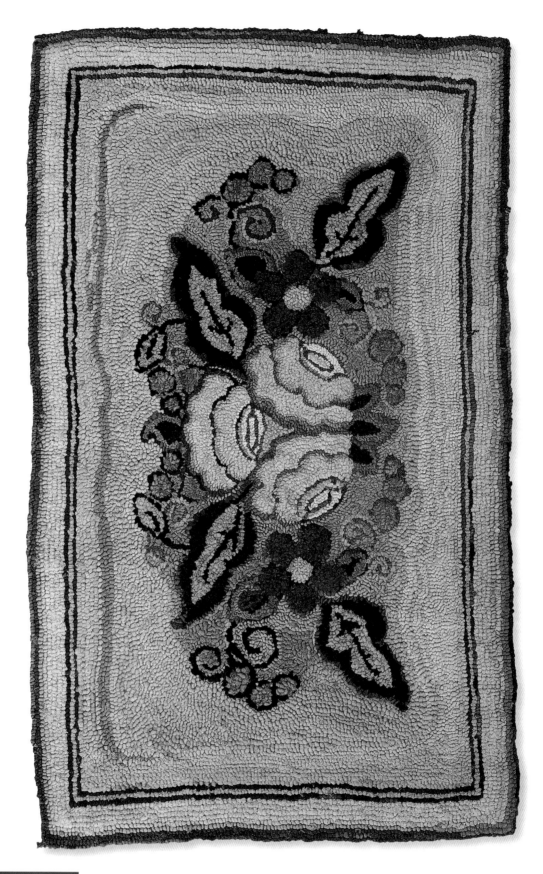

Floral Trio, 21" x 34". Designer unknown. From the author's collection. There is much I enjoy about this rug: the assortment of fabrics used for the background and the way it is hooked, the simple lines that create a border, the lightness of the center flowers, and the dark edges of the leaves. (Check out page 64 in Chapter 6, Backgrounds, to see how Irene Shell of Woodinville, Washington, hooked this same pattern.)

REIMAGINED RUG **Floral Trio,** 32" x 50". Hooked by Laurel Starks of Stow, Ohio. I was surprised when Laurel chose this pattern (it was one of the smallest rugs and she usually hooks large rugs). But I wasn't surprised when I saw it finished. She took the center design, doubled it, made a few more changes, and then added a shell or lamb's tongue border to complete it. I love the use of the lighter small flowers and the way she highlighted the two bouquets.

REIMAGINED RUG **Floral Trio,** 22" x 35". Hooked by Lauren Smesny Wade of Kingwood, Texas. Yes, I love purples, so you know this rendition was one I was delighted to see. Lauren gave much more detail to each of the larger flowers and her background is a good combination of echoing and squiggles, which keeps your eye moving. The few lines of straight-line hooking create a simple but effective border for this rug.

Geometric Leaf, 17" x 33". Designer unknown. From the author's collection. This piece appealed to me because some of the diamonds repeat a design while the others do not, which makes this rug more whimsical. The soft colors are eye-catching even with the black scattered throughout.

Geometric Leaf, 19" x 33". Hooked by Dorothy Delaune of Covington, Louisiana. Dorothy did a great job with color. She balances the darkness of the brown in the design by carrying it to the outer border. She used a fabulous fabric for the outer edge and used it again when binding the rug.

Scrolls Galore, 24" x 36". Designer unknown. From the author's collection. When I saw this rug, I had to have it. I couldn't imagine what the rug hooker was thinking when she put those red lips right in the center of this rug. It contrasted with the beautiful scrolls. It was almost like two different people hooked this one rug. One scroll in particular shows that if you run out of one wool, it is fine to simply pick another one and keep hooking.

Scrolls Galore, 25" x 37". Hooked by Carrie Martin of Covington, Louisiana. Carrie took this simple design and made it a beautiful rug. The red in the flowers is effectively repeated in the scrolls. I love the use of the various greens in the central piece and in the scrolls. It gives an iridescence to the design. Note the beautiful fabric used for the background.

Opposite page, top: Antique Flower Basket, 24" x 34". Designer unknown. From the author's collection. This rug is an excellent example of why we no longer use burlap for the foundation and why we no longer simply turn the edges under to bind the rug. It's interesting to see how the different blacks in the background have faded over time. When the rug was first made, the blacks would have most likely appeared the same value. Also, the flowers and the corner ears have faded from a bright color to the dulled pinks. This was a free pattern in my book, *Creating an Antique Look in Hand-Hooked Rugs,* Rug Hooking *magazine, 2008.*

Opposite page, bottom: Antique Flower Basket, 24" x 34". Hooked by the author. The antique rug was replicated, but I added color by using leftover pieces for the flowers and leaves. With time and wear, these will fade, but for now, it works well in a hallway in my home. Flower baskets are one of the more popular old designs.

BELOW: Antique Flower Basket, 24" x 34". Hooked by Carol Daugherty of South Bend, Indiana. Carol took the original design and made it much more interesting by dropping two of the flowers, adding berries, losing the handle of the basket, and adding squiggles in place of the corner ears. I really love how she hooked the oval surrounding the design—note all the action going on in that small space.

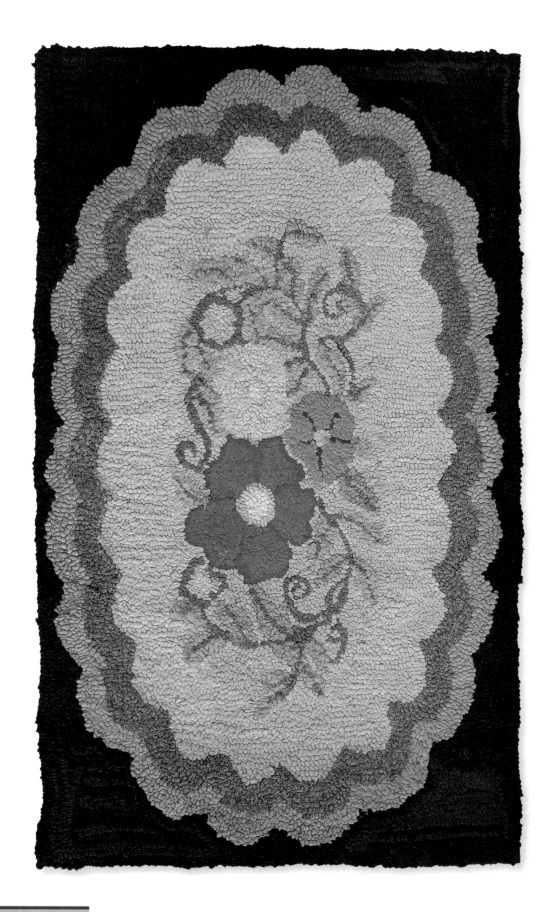

Spring, 23" x 37". Designer unknown. From the author's collection. I love the whimsical use of red, pink, and orange, and I also especially appreciate the unbalanced use of those colors. Both of these things are difficult for most modern rug hookers to accomplish.

Spring, 30" x 44". Hooked by Sally Schill of Columbus, Ohio. Sally turned the simple design into a lovely rug with blue, purple, and red flowers. While the leaves are gorgeous, they do not outshine the flowers.

CHAPTER TWO

What's the Story?

A Brief History of Rug Hooking

Primitive rugs hooked today pay homage and tribute to the antique rugs we may be lucky enough to find, see, or even own. As we study these antiques, we see a direct line from the antique rugs to the creation of our own primitive rugs. When teaching and talking, I find that I frequently use the terms *primitive* and *antique* interchangeably because in my mind they are that close in colors, subject matter, and design. It is mainly age that separates them. Today we have the opportunity to make beautiful primitive rugs based on our study of antique rugs. But of course, the antique rugs were created long ago; these days, we are creating primitive rugs which one day will be called antiques. Today we simply call them primitives.

Our ancestors made use of any fabric they had access to, but usually they used worn out or outgrown clothing. They often used woolen underwear, blankets, and uniforms, and they were not concerned if it was woolen fabric or something else. Remember—these early rugs were utilitarian.

Although the rugs expressed some artistic ability, they were more important for their intended use—to cover dirt floors or drafty wooden flooring or to provide bedding covers to keep the family warm. Even if they were not considered works of art, their creators took pride in their work by making beautiful loops and using colors they liked or happened to have on hand to make something that was not only useful and beautiful, but would also last for years. These rugs were works of love. Few of the earliest rugs survived precisely because they were not considered works of art; they were utilitarian. They were one form of creativity expressed by the women of that time, but unfortunately they were ravaged by wear, dirt, light, and time.

ELEMENTS OF PRIMITIVE RUGS

Primitive rugs will vary in topic, size, shape, width of fabric strips, and even materials used, but they all tend to evoke a feeling of warmth and comfort. What makes a rug primitive? If you ask ten people, you most likely will get ten different responses—and all will be correct. Most people will agree that primitive rugs employ simplicity of design, use of soft and somewhat muted colors, use of unusual colors, and odd placement of some colors. They also usually include bizarre background hooking patterns, the use of wider strips of fabric, and occasionally a lack of respect for perspective, scale, balance, or proportion. That makes a rug whimsical and charming. To a primitive rug hooker, the rug seems to speak to the soul. It's usually not one specific object or color that appeals to the viewer, but rather the overall effect or tone of the rug.

Vintage Blooms, 36" x 72". Designed and hooked by Theresa Rapstine Schafer of Denver, Colorado. She was inspired by an old rug (circa 1900) that is the property of The Society for the Preservation of New England Antiquities at the Beauport-Sleeper McCann House in Gloucester, Massachusetts. This beautiful rug contains hand-dyed and as-is wool as well as recycled fabric with cuts from 8.5 to 10. RICHARD SCHAFER

Cora and Bentley, 29" x 41". Antique rug owned by Barbara Carroll of Ligonier, Pennsylvania. Note the various sections and colors used in the background. The sporadic placement of colors in the triangles increases our interest in this rug. DEB BURCIN

ORIGINS AND HISTORY

The origins of rug hooking are at best murky. Some historical publications date the craft to Scandinavian countries in the 1700s. Some state it began in England in the early 1800s, while another source asserts it began as early as the 1300s in Egypt. And we have all heard the tale of sailors fashioning a nail into a hook and using materials aboard ship to while away both time and boredom. However, most historians tend to agree that the most likely root of rug hooking was in North America in the early 1800s.

By the 1830s, the craft was definitely ensconced in one particular region—Nova Scotia, Newfoundland, and upper Maine. It spread in the 1860s throughout New England and into Pennsylvania, and by the 1890s, rug hooking had spread nationwide and patterns could even be purchased from Sears or Montgomery Ward.

Interest in rug hooking declined soon thereafter only to be revived again in the 1920s through the actions of a group of interior designers who were pushing a resurgence and revival of decorative arts in America. The rugs were referred to as "Colonial Arts" by several well-known designers even though they were not hooked or used during that time period. We owe that group of designers much, because through their actions another resurgence began. Not only did consumers begin buying newly hooked rugs, but collectors became interested in collecting old hooked rugs. Rug hooking even became a staple in parts of Arkansas, Louisiana, and Texas after the 1920s. Mrs. Harry King was one of the instrumental people in that region, just as Pearl McGown was in the Northeast. Now, rug hookers can be found everywhere. We owe a debt of gratitude to our forbearers who kept this art alive and growing.

Cora and Bentley, 29" x 41". Hooked by Barbara Carroll of Ligonier, Pennsylvania. I love how Barb moved the purple throughout this rug, but the blue horse is the crowning touch. Pattern available from Woolley Fox.

Another layer of cloth was sewn to the back of this rug. Additional backing shows how much this antique rug was loved. Someone did her best to save the rug from complete deterioration.

Homeward Bound, 34" x 22". Hooked by Lisanne Miller of Canton, Mississippi. This pattern from New England Heritage Series is available from P is for Primitive. The ship heading home is indicative of many of the early patterns, which were composed of scenes familiar to those on the east coast of early America.

Before 1850, rugs were hooked on loosely woven homespun linen. After 1850, burlap was mass produced and became a less expensive option in the United States. It was easier to buy and much easier to hook on than homespun linen, so rug hooking became more popular. Before 1870, most of the hooked rugs were original designs drawn by the rug hooker or a family member. After 1870, several people, including Edward Sands Frost, were selling preprinted patterns and rug hooking became even more popular. Although the availability of printed patterns limited some creativity, the influx of patterns didn't stop ingenuity. Some rug hookers would "borrow" part of a pattern design from a neighbor or friend and add their own center or border. If you are interested in the history of rug hooking, pick up any one of the numerous books on the topic, including the series by W. W. Kent. You should also visit the Hooked Rug Museum of North America in Halifax, Nova Scotia.

Close-up of corner of *Fern with Scrolls*. Note the variety of fabrics used.

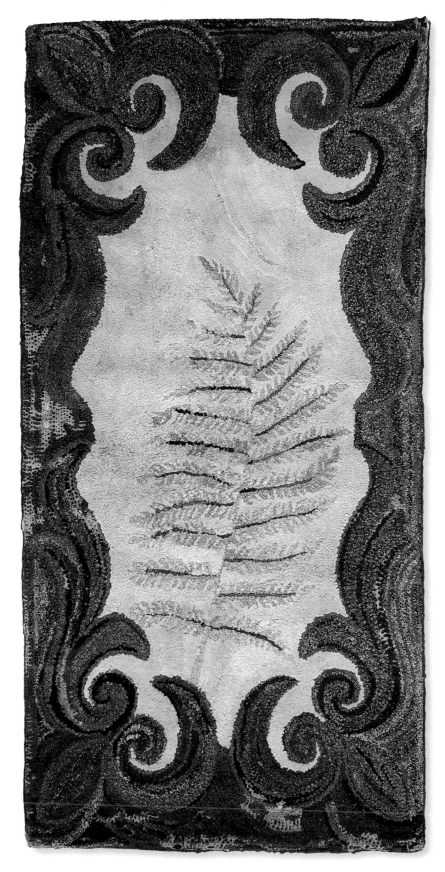

Fern with Scrolls, 30" x 60". From the author's collection. Circa 1880, designer unknown. The border design is a much more professional design than the simple center field. It appears the rug hooker had the commercially created border pattern and decided to add one giant fern leaf in the center. This is what makes the rug so interesting to modern day collectors.

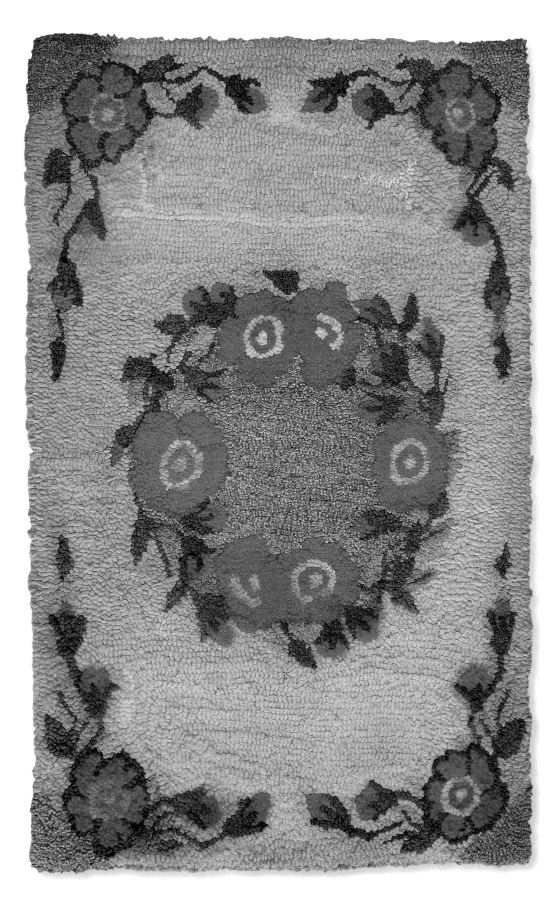

Crown of Roses, 26"x 40". Designer unknown. Early 1900s, located in Pennsylvania. From the author's collection. Note the interesting, irregular transition from the center background to the outer background and the treatment of the corners. The red fabric may be from red flannel underwear.

CURRENT STATUS OF PRIMITIVE RUG HOOKING

Rug hooking in general has had numerous ebbs and flows in popularity. Currently it appears to be on an upswing again with even younger rug hookers taking up the art. Primitive rug hooking appeals to more rug hookers now for several reasons. It doesn't take a lot of equipment to start—a hook, a hoop, scissors, and a beginner's kit. Of course, the more one gets into the craft, the more—and better—equipment you usually want. Rug hooking is also relatively easy to learn. The basics are simple and are quickly recognized as properly done. Primitive rug hooking uses wider strips of fabric; thus, the rug hooker accomplishes more in less time than if she were hooking a finer cut piece. Primitives seem to work the best in our current home décor. Most of us are less formal now, and primitive rugs warm up any room.

The primitive rugs I hook use random widths of wool strips, including some that are hand cut or cut and torn. Varying the strip width automatically creates more interest and makes the loops look different than if they were all the same width. If the strip is wider, the beauty of the fabric can be admired. Although most of us strive for perfection, the height of the loops does not need to be identical. Randomness is truly better in primitive rugs. When inspecting an old hooked rug, notice how the taller loops fall over onto their neighbors.

I only use as-is textured wool and have done so since the early 1990s because it better replicates the old look. To my eye, spot-dyed wool is too shocking for a primitive rug, so I never use it in my rugs. Over-dyed and married textures are easier to incorporate with as-is textures. I started hooking and collecting wools in 1980 and many of my favorite pieces of fabric are from my early days of gathering recycled wool from friends and thrift shops. Even with all the new, exciting textures on the market now, my private stash from old recycled clothing is still my favorite and hidden from public viewing. But remember, you are creating your own piece of art, so use wools that are beautiful and comforting to your eye.

Botanical Runner, 20" x 60". Hooked by Corrine Watts of Washington, D.C. While most primitive rug hookers would think this rug is too bright, if you study old primitive rugs you will discover they were hooked in much brighter colors than they now appear to be. This is Corrine's first attempt at #8 cut, and in years, it will be a great antique. So don't be afraid to use color. Pattern is available from Main Street Rugs. SHARON TURNER/IMAGES BY SHARON

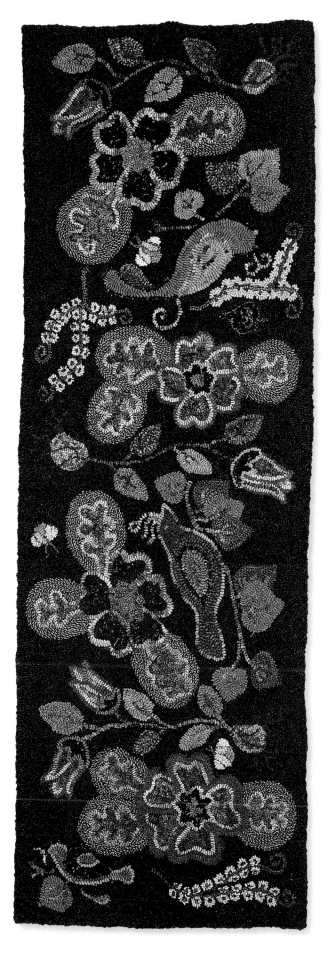

CHAPTER THREE

Techniques for Primitive Rugs

Learning to hook primitive rugs is very similar to learning to hook any rug. The basic techniques are the same, but we have to pay attention to a few special considerations that will identify our rugs as primitive.

For most people, the best way to learn to rug hook is to have an instructor or a friend demonstrate the basic method. While the technique is very simple, people learn differently. Some need only to be told how to do something, some need to see it done, and some need to attempt it under a watchful eye. However, most of us are kinesthetic learners—we want all three options! And sometimes repetition helps us really conquer a technique. Or consider attending a rug camp to learn from an instructor and

Popular foundations for rug hooking. The smaller square (left) is rug warp. Long rectangle is monk's cloth. Larger square (right) is linen.

Out in the Garden, 20" x 38". Hooked by Jane Aebie of Chardon, Ohio. Designed and available from Maggie Bonanomi. This is a great pattern for the beginner as well as a more advanced rug hooker. The sparkling movement of the blue fabric keeps your eye moving across the rug.

books or magazine articles available. Times have changed, and now it's even easier to teach yourself: buy a video, watch YouTube instructions, or check out rug hooking websites to learn basic and advanced techniques. A great number of wonderful books and a couple of magazines are available to help you learn the basics or improve your technique.

Techniques of rug hooking are as diverse as the number of individuals hooking. There are different hooks, different ways to hold each hook, and different directions to hook. But a few items are common no matter which way you hook. You need a comfortable, well-lighted location, a good hook, a pattern you like, good wool, and a frame to hold your foundation taut.

I think linen is the best foundation to use. It will last for hundreds of years, doesn't have an odor, is soft to the touch, and holds its form. Some rug hookers prefer monk's cloth, which is a cotton product, and they obtain good results with it. And others prefer rug warp, another cotton product that is a little stiffer than monk's cloth because of the way it is woven. Although you can hook a primitive on rug warp, I don't suggest you try it unless you are using smaller strips instead of wider cuts. Very few current day rug hookers in the United States use burlap—the foundation that made rug hooking very popular in the latter part of the 1800s. Burlap has a short life span, has a distinct odor, and is a little more difficult to hook than linen. I suggest that you see, touch, and hook with all of these and decide which one you prefer. Most pattern makers will print on a variety of foundations. I feel so strongly about linen that I even suggest beginners start on linen, although burlap kits are much less expensive than linen kits. If it's easier to hook in the beginning, a new student is more likely to keep hooking, and using linen is one simple step that makes rug hooking more fun from the start.

the other students in your class. Camps can be found in all price ranges, covering many different techniques, and in all parts of the United States and Canada. Some camps offer beginner classes.

Many people are self-taught and do a wonderful job without any assistance. So don't be afraid to attempt to hook on your own. In the old days, you could easily learn by reading one of the numerous

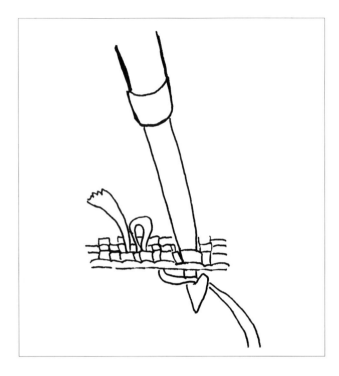

HOW TO HOOK

The technique for primitive rug hooking is simple and can be conquered by most in just a few minutes. First, it's a good idea to have your linen foundation on a frame so it is kept taut and your hands are not trying to balance your hooking. If necessary, you can use a good quality quilting hoop and balance it on the edge of a table and on your wrist, keeping the fingers of your left hand completely under the foundation.

Hold a strip of wool underneath the linen in your left hand, and with the right hand, push the hook through a hole in the linen. Allow the hook to catch or grab the strip of wool, and pull the end or the tail to the top side of the linen. Don't twist or wrap the strip of wool around the hook like you would if you were crocheting. If you wrap it on the hook, you will most likely end up with bumps and lumps on the back side of your foundation. We want the back to be smooth and flat with no lumps or bumps. Push your hook into the next hole and pull the strip up again. You will create a beautiful loop by gently rolling the hook toward the tail you pulled up previously.

With the next loop you pull up, you need to skip a couple of holes. Don't try to fill every hole or even every other hole if you are hooking primitives. You don't need to count the holes you skip. You simply want each loop to lightly touch the neighboring loop. The wider the strip of wool you are using, the more holes you need to skip. The loops should not be crowded together like sardines in a can. You should

be able to see the curve on the top of the loop. The loops need to breathe with that extra space so that you can see all the wonderful colors in your textured wool.

When you finish one strip of wool, pull the tail up to the top. Start the next strip of wool in that same hole. If you notice that your loops are coming out, make sure you are rolling your hook toward the previously made loop. If you pull straight up or away from your last loop, you may pull out the previous loop.

In general, your loops should be pulled as high as your fabric strip is wide. To gauge your height, place one strip on its side near your latest row of hooking. Why do you need to pull it that high? Doing so allows you to more easily see the beauty of the textured wools you are using, and a longer term benefit is that the rug will wear well. Also you most likely will hook faster and cover the area more quickly because pulling the loops higher opens them up so they cover more space. You will also use less fabric because you are skipping more holes.

Most people tend to pull the strips too low, which hides the colors and texture of the wool. When you push your hook into the linen, push it all the way in so that you create a larger hole for the strip of wool to be pulled through more easily. The hand underneath doesn't help the wool onto the hook. It serves to hold the wool strip flat as you pull it up with the hook in order to keep it from twisting or making a bump or lump on the back of the linen. The back of the rug needs to be smooth so the rug will wear well.

Remember to skip holes and let your loops breathe. It is almost impossible to pull your loops too high or to skip too many holes. I have only had one student who pulled her strips higher than was necessary, but her rugs look fabulous and are great to walk on. She just knows that she will use much more wool than most rug hookers will. Your eye will quickly let you know and you can make corrections if the spacing is too great. It is very easy to fill too many holes or to pack your hooking, especially when you are a beginner. If you pack your loops, your rug won't wear as well, will take much longer to hook, and will use much more wool. So it's better to learn the best way to hook at the beginning of your career. Your technique will improve with each rug hooking session.

Crossed Pineapples, 48" x 48". Hooked by Kristi Roberts of Houston, Texas. I love how each of the pineapples is treated individually . . . different fabrics and different tops. While the background is light, note that the outer border is a shade darker than the center. Pattern available from Vermont Folk Rugs.

HOOKING TECHNIQUES FOR MORE PRIMITIVE EFFECT

When hooking a primitive rug, don't bog yourself down worrying about the irregular height of your loops. You will get better with practice and time. And if you don't, it doesn't matter. Primitive rugs are unlike tapestry hooking. We don't need the loops to be perfect. While we are discussing perfection, remember primitive rugs are an expression of your personal taste. You are not or should not be making them to impress others. It doesn't matter if your star has sharp points or curved points; as long as your brain recognizes it is a star, all is well.

Laszlo, 31" x 40". Hooked by Crystal Brown of Washington, Pennsylvania. Note the imperfect fence posts. This rug is proof you don't need a ton of colors to have a great rug. I love his blue face. This pattern is based on an antique coverlet and is available from Woolley Fox.

Hearth Floral, 16" x 51". Hooked by Dea Olson of Topeka, Kansas. This design is from an old rug owned by the author. The designer is unknown. Various widths of wool were used to complete this gorgeous rug. The leaves show life and movement.

The most important thing to remember is don't pack your loops; let them barely touch each other. Leave spaces between your rows of hooking as well as between your loops. You can offset each row of hooking for a more even look, but I don't like to waste the time it takes to do that. I let my hook decide where it needs to go. The only time you might want to be more careful about the pattern lines is when you are hooking geometrics. If you hook on the line one place and outside the line in another, the pattern will not be accurate. But if it's primitive, it's okay that way.

QUICK TIPS FOR PRIMITIVES

1. When hooking a circle, it's more natural and okay to fill more holes than you would when hooking a straight line.
2. Most rug hookers work right to left or top to bottom. The direction that works best for you is the right one.
3. Keep the hooking on the back of the foundation nice and smooth and without bumps if the rug will be on the floor.
4. Pull your loops as high as the strip is wide.
5. Don't pack your loops. The wider the strip is, the more holes you need to skip.
6. If an instructor tells you there is only one way to do something, find another instructor.
7. When hooking smaller motifs, it's easier to outline first then fill.
8. To keep the design from getting too large, hook on or inside the drawn lines.

USE VARYING WIDTHS OF WOOL STRIPS

Once you have your technique perfected, you should practice with different width strips. Most primitive hookers like #8, 8.5, 9, 9.5, 10, or wider. You will soon find which size you prefer, but don't be surprised if your preferred size changes over time. It's important to be comfortable using different sizes of strips as you may occasionally hook a design that requires narrow strips for more detail.

If you use narrow strips mixed with wider strips, just pull the narrow strip as high as you would pull the wider one so it doesn't get lost. Varying strip widths can help make a rug look more primitive. The wider strips will be of more interest as it shows more of the colors of the textured wool you are using. Most primitive rug hookers use long strips of wool in order to have fewer stops and starts and fewer tails, and you can hook faster with fewer stops and starts. But there is no correct answer; use the length of strip that is most comfortable to you. Especially when hooking backgrounds or borders, I prefer strips 24 inches and longer. The more experienced you become, the longer strips you will like.

Varying the width of the strips of wool creates more interest in your rug. One suggestion is to use a narrower strip to outline a design then fill it with a wider strip. The widest strips are best used for the border, especially if you are hooking in straight lines with a large plaid. If you want your beauty line or break line to make a statement, use the widest strip there. If you have a fabric you love and want it to be the star of your rug, use a wider strip than the others. Don't be afraid to mix the width of your cut wool. Add hand-cut strips for even more fun.

Summer Delight, 14" x 20". Designed and hooked by the author. One small checked fabric was used for the break line, while another small checked fabric was used for the vine. Keep your eyes open for small checks for your stash, for they can be used in a myriad of ways.

BEAUTY LINES OR BREAK LINES

Unlike some handwork, you can start wherever you like and you can jump from one section to another. Most of us will hook the design first. And you can jump around even when hooking the design. It's always best to hook at least one row of background around your design as you hook each element. This serves two purposes: it allows you to see if your background choice will work, and it helps reduce the amount of background you will have to hook later. Many rug hookers get bored when hooking the background.

Generally, a pattern will have a border. The line between the background and the border is referred to as a beauty line or a break line. Although this is only a simple line on your pattern, it is very important as it separates the interior design from the border. You have several options:

- you can simply change fabrics at that point and not do anything specific with the actual line,

- you can pick a bold fabric that has nothing to do with the rest of the rug,
- or you can pick a fabric that has some of the colors of the main design.

Most primitive rug hookers will use a fabric that distinctly separates the two areas. The line creates a break. Small checks and colorful plaids can work well for this single row of hooking.

Experiment with different fabrics; if you don't like what you hook, it is easy to remove since it's only one row. This may be the perfect place to use that strange piece of fabric that you don't know how to use.

TOOLS—OPTIONS AND ADVANTAGES

The market is full of great options when it comes to rug hooking tools. Many styles of hooks, frames, and cutters abound over a wide price range. These items are such personal decisions that I suggest that you try before you buy. You can start with inexpensive hooks, a quilting hoop, and regular scissors, but if

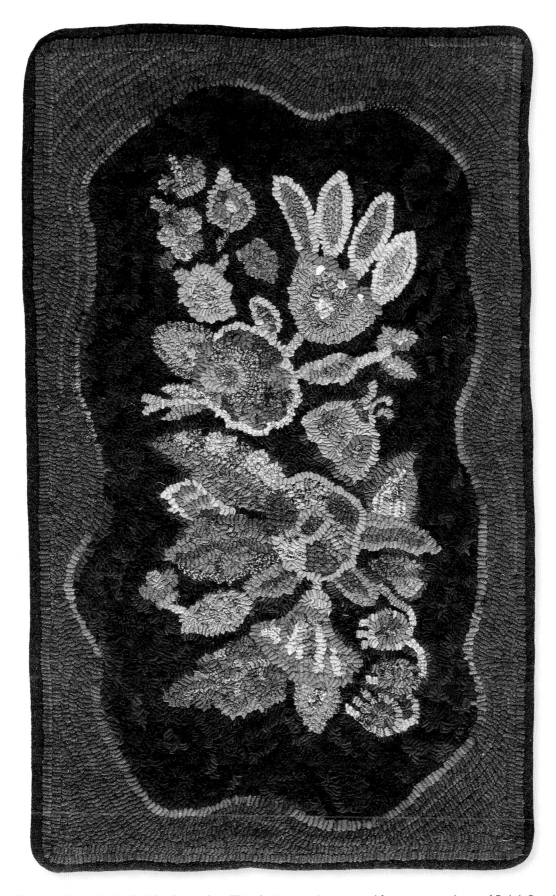

Burnham's Floral, 36" x 26". Hooked by the author. This design was interpreted from copper plates of Ralph Burnham. The cut-and-tear method was used for all of the wool except for the outer border. It doesn't matter if all the strips are the same width. The pattern from New England Heritage Society is available from P is for Primitive.

you like this art, better equipment will make it easier and much more fun. Check ads in *Rug Hooking* magazine and *ATHA Magazine* and online websites to see what is available.

If you are in a class, ask your instructor what she likes and why she likes it. Notice what other students are using. You can later pass down your beginner equipment to another person when you upgrade your own equipment. You can usually try different equipment from friends, teachers, or campmates. At camp, ask people why they like a particular item or what they don't like about it. You will find most rug hookers are very willing to share.

You may make a mistake in a purchase, but you can always find someone else who will want what you don't like. My suggestion is this: if you can afford to buy the best equipment on the market when you first start rug hooking, do it. The best tools will make your rug hooking more enjoyable and you won't struggle.

CUT-AND-TEAR METHOD

The cutter is one of the most expensive pieces of equipment you may buy. But if you wish, you can hook like the ladies did in the 1800s and not use a cutter. Some people use a rotary mat and cutter like quilters use, but I prefer to use the older method called cut-and-tear or hand-torn. And yes, it's that simple. You basically make a short cut or snip in your fabric, usually parallel to the selvage. Then you tear the fabric. If you like the width, then hook with it. If

it's too wide, take your scissors and simply cut it in half lengthwise. It is not necessary to have a straight line when cutting since you have a torn edge on one side, which is on the straight of the grain. The fact that the torn strips are not all equal in width creates more interest in the rug. I find this technique peaceful, and I will often mix torn strips into a rug with cutter-created strips. The tighter the fabric is woven, the narrower you will be able to tear it. If the fabric is loosely woven, tear a strip twice as wide as you need, then merely cut it in half with scissors. Try it; you might enjoy the process.

HOW MUCH WOOL DO I NEED?

If you are doing a primitive, you need not worry about this. If you run out of one fabric, simply add another fabric. Each rug hooker's technique varies based on how high and how tightly packed the loops are. However, a good rule to remember is that the wider your strips are, the more wool you will need. If you are using a #8 cut or wider, you plan to use a piece of wool six times the surface area you are hooking. This is easier than it sounds. Simply place six layers of fabric on top of the design you want to hook. If you want to see how much one piece of fabric will hook, fold it in half and then fold it into thirds. That will give you six layers and that is the area it will cover when hooked.

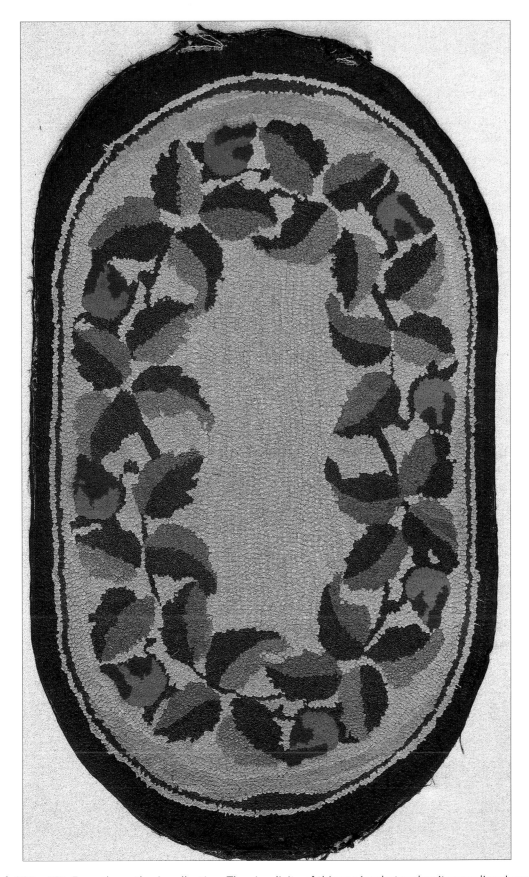

Rosebud, 30" x 60". From the author's collection. The simplicity of this rug is what makes it appealing. I can imagine the rug hooker gathering her wools and trying to make them stretch to complete the rug. At first glance it appears she only used two greens for the leaves. Look again and you will see three used randomly. The rosebuds are hooked very simply, but there is no doubt in your mind what they represent.

CHAPTER FOUR

Great Fabrics for Primitive Rugs

Close-up of flower in **Antique Cornucopia.** Hooked by the author. Note all the different colors used, from orange to pink to red to purple. To hook a red flower doesn't mean you need to use only red fabrics.

Choosing fabrics for your primitive rug deserves careful consideration. Your choice of fabric and the source of that fabric are important identifiers of primitive rugs. Fabric choice, combined with hooking technique and design, make primitive rugs stand out from any other category of rug hooking.

VALUE OF USING OTHER FABRICS

Today most of us prefer to not only use 100% wool, but we actually shy away from recycled wools salvaged from old clothing. In the early 1980s, if a primitive rug hooker wanted great textured wools like plaids, tweeds, checks, stripes, and herringbones, she was relegated to hunting thrift shops and friends' closets for these wonderful wools because most of the wools processed for rug hooking were solids and only a few basic textured samples were available. Now we have a fabulous array of new textured wools to stockpile our rug hooking shelves. But by using antique fabrics or recycled pieces you will create work that will stand out among others in a good way. Not only will your piece be special, but it will also contain the history of the fabrics used. You are recycling. By utilizing different weights or thicknesses of wool in your rug, you will produce a rug more like those of the past when the rug hooker didn't worry about the fabric she used. She was more interested in finding the color that she wanted for that space.

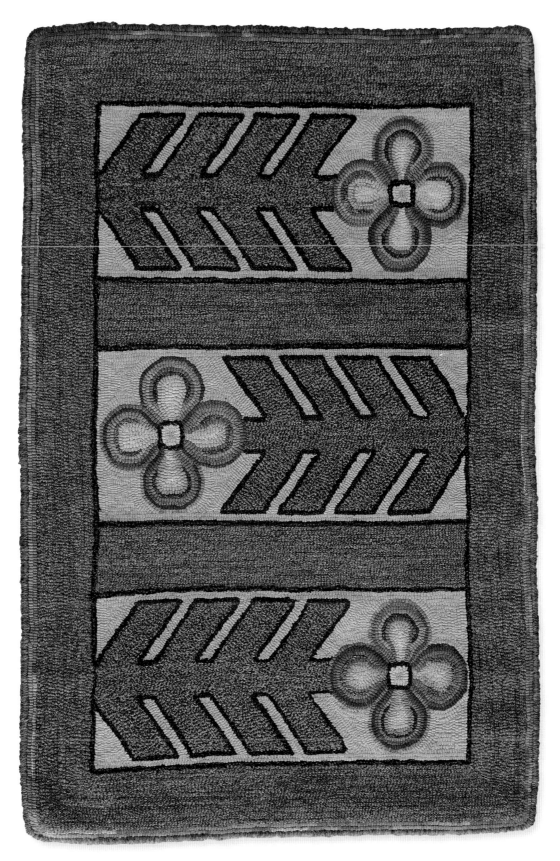

Swedish Rose, 25" x 36". Hooked by the author. This was my first adventure, in the early 1980s, into using recycled wool. One fabric was from a man's jacket and the other was from a Pendleton skirt. Both were used as-is. The orangey-peach fabric was purchased from a local teacher; it was an over-dyed recycled piece also. The pattern is from Hook and Needle Gallery, Chagrin Falls, Ohio.

Antique Welcome Bowl, 20" x 34". Designer unknown. From the author's collection. There are several intriguing things about this antique rug: the floating bowl, the disjointed flowers, and the unrecognizable letters at the base.

RECYCLED FABRIC

Some of us enjoy using pieces of recycled wool in our work. Because those wools are limited, many hookers don't have ready access to them. The rug using recycled fabrics will have a more distinctive look due to the unusual fabrics, whether it is the pattern, texture, or thickness of the fabric. The original antique welcome rug shown here includes fabrics other than wool, including rayon and gabardine.

My copy of this rug contains many recycled pieces that I have hoarded since the early 1980s. However, some new fabrics are scattered in the flowers, leaves, and bowl. Those new fabrics are not wool, they are cotton flannel. It is a little thinner than wool but hooks the same and looks great. It will not repel dirt as well as wool does, so I would suggest not using cotton flannel in a rug for a high traffic area, but it's fine for pillows, wall hangings, or tabletop pieces. The background and the border are all recycled wools, mainly from skirts and Pendleton shirts or bathrobes. I used seven different fabrics in the border. Of course, I could not resist using another old fabric—antique paisley.

PAISLEY, LINSEY-WOOLSEY, RAYON, AND SILK

The oldest recycled fabric I love to incorporate in primitive rugs is antique paisley. Even with specially dyed fabrics, you cannot duplicate the result achieved

Note the various colors and designs of the antique shawls.

with antique paisley. The paisley I use comes from shawls produced between 1830 and 1880 in England, Scotland, and France. These paisley shawls are not repairable, nor are they historically important or rare. Please do not destroy a shawl without having a knowledgeable person evaluate it. Just because it has a few holes, doesn't mean it is a "cutter." Also, not all paisleys are strong enough to be used in rug hooking. While the most dominant colors used in paisley shawls were orange and black, the shawls came in all colors.

Cynthia's Antique Welcome Bowl, 20" x 34". Hooked by the author. This newly hooked primitive rug uses recycled fabrics, cotton flannel, and antique paisley. When you hook an antique design, hook it your way and use fabrics you want. Don't just try to replicate the original. Create your own rug!

Close-up of *Pear Tree,* page 81. Hooked by the author. This bird uses only antique paisley shawls from my private collection of cutters. Purple and teal are rare colors in shawls—these are both from shawls I cut up before I became a student of antique paisley and learned the history and differences in paisleys. Adapted from a Notforgotten Farm/Lori Brechlin design by Spruce Ridge Studios © 2009.

Dancing Boot, 11" x 13". Designed and hooked by the author. This boot is hooked completely in antique paisley. The blue and white piece running down the seam of the boot is from a Kirking shawl (the name comes from the German *kirche* for "church"). The Kirking shawls were normally worn by mothers when their child was baptized. They also were used by brides in the 1860s and were considered part of the trousseau. These shawls were proud possessions passed from one family member to another. They are also called Norwich shawls.

HOW TO HOOK WITH ANTIQUE PAISLEY

1. Buy good paisley from a knowledgeable person.
2. Use a #8 cut or wider for best results.
3. Only cut what you will immediately use.
4. Pull strips high and skip fewer holes than normal.
5. Make sure the woven side is on top, not the thread side.
6. Paisley can be hand cut, but be sure to stay straight by tearing one edge.
7. I cut my paisley one size wider than the rest of the strips in the rug.
8. You can cut a wide strip and fold it in half for a narrower strip.
9. For extra strength, hook the paisley on top of another strip of wool.

Linsey-woolsey is a coarse fabric usually made with a linen warp and a wool weft. Sometimes it was created with cotton and wool. It has a different feel or texture and is a little more difficult to hook, but it will give a great look that is different than 100% wool. Pieces of linsey-woolsey from an antique blanket I received from an antique dealer friend were used in the background of *Hannah's Barnyard*.

Hannah's Barnyard,
30" x 51". Designed and hooked by the author from templates provided by Barb Carroll and Jule Marie Smith. Linsey-woolsey from a blanket was mixed with the various wools in the background. Many of the designs use antique paisley.

Trio of Circles (above) and **Simply Eight** (opposite page)**,** from the author's collection. These two old rugs are constructed entirely of silk and rayon. The fabric could have come from silk or rayon stockings, print dresses, or underwear. From a distance they both appear to be hooked from wool until you get close enough to touch. They are both on a burlap base and have held up very well.

MAGIC FABRICS TO CREATE SPECIAL EFFECTS

The fabrics in this photo can do much of the work for you if you just allow your imagination to flow. The red and purple stripe is vibrant and wild, but imagine it cut and kept in separate color families. You could create a simple and elegant flower by using a separate color in each petal. To tone down the chroma, use olive green and dark gold in the center of the flower.

This small check with red is great for a break line or a beauty line between the border and the background.

The green plaid can easily create a beautiful leaf. Use the lighter section for one side of the leaf and the darker section on the other side. Or you could cut the strips and mix them randomly.

The lighter plaid is one of my favorites to use for stems, veins, or the single outline of a flower center.

Because it contains various colors, it can be used in many ways.

The purple and green piece will make beautiful primitive leaves whether it is used randomly or separated by using the more purple section for flowers.

The orange and teal plaid is great for flower centers and also replicates the look of antique paisley, if you don't want to use the real thing.

The red plaid with gold in it is one of my favorite reds. It has life and works great in flowers, berries, and Santa's suit!

The multi-striped fabric is perfect for outlining stars or for filling them completely. For a more varied effect, cut it across the grain if you are hooking with #8 cut or wider.

PLAIDS AND CHECKS

1. Large plaids are perfect to use in borders.
2. Small, muted, darker checks are great for the roof of a house or building.
3. Purple plaids and checks are easier to use than solid purple. And every rug needs some purple!
4. Multicolored checks are perfect for outlining flowers or for individual petals.
5. Use tiny checks with white for eyes.
6. Small checks work well for flower centers and stems.
7. Colorful checks or plaids are great for a break line or a beauty line.

LARGE PLAIDS

Some rug hookers ignore large plaids, but I love them and you will too once you use them. The rose and green combination plaid on the left will make a beautiful flower with the darker strip. Gorgeous soft primitive leaves will result from the lighter strip, especially if you add more olive green strips. The plaid on the right makes the most interesting background without the rug hooker having to dye or think about which fabric to use. So be smart and gather some large plaids for your stash. Large plaids containing various colors are also perfect to use in borders. It is best if the plaids duplicate some of the colors used in the design of your rug.

Keep your eyes open for unusual pieces of fabric, whether they be unusual due to color, texture, pattern, cutting requirements, unusual prints, or rough textures. These interesting pieces will make your rug different from those of other rug hookers who are unwilling to experiment.

LOOSELY WOVEN FABRICS

Loosely woven fabrics should not be ignored. Here are two samples composed of silk, linen, and wool that appear to be too loosely woven for a rug hooker to consider using. But once they are washed and dried, they are perfect for a primitive rug. These two pieces also make beautiful snow in #9 cuts, as seen in *Kris Kringle* on page 86.

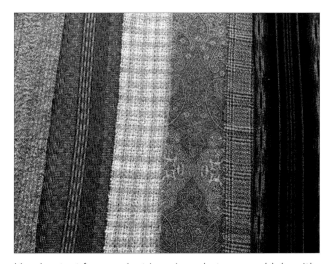

Here's a test for you. Just imagine what you could do with these special fabrics.

USING NUMEROUS FABRICS IN THE SAME MOTIF

While hooking primitive rugs, we don't restrict ourselves to the use of only one fabric in one area. It is more fun and interesting to use as many different fabrics in one area as possible. Don't let a small area make you think that one or two fabrics are adequate. The more the merrier! Pay attention to value and/or color and you will have a great rug. If the range of value is too strong your rug may be choppy looking and not appealing to your eye. I very seldom use one fabric for the background. In order not to be bored, I like to see how many different fabrics I can use in the background. (The record now is fifteen different wools, but the normal count is more like nine.) Here's another benefit of using more than one fabric: if you run out of wool, you don't need to worry about matching fabrics.

AS-IS VERSUS DYED FABRICS

I prefer using as-is wools, but I happen to have an amazing variety and a large collection in which to hunt. The reason for using as-is, textured wools instead of dyed wool is simple. Because of the way the fabric is woven with a multitude of colored threads, the colors are there, but they are muted. The colors of textured wools automatically soften the rug and make it more primitive in appearance. The over-dyed pieces will be more stark when compared to as-is textured pieces. If you need to use over-dyed fabrics to get the color you want, choose a piece that is softer and more muted and not high chroma. Search first for your colors in textured, as-is fabrics.

LET THE WOOL TALK TO YOU: TEXTURES FOR PRIMITIVE RUGS

1 When you are hooking with all these wonderful textures, don't just outline with one fabric and fill with another. Vary not only the fabrics you use to fill, but also use several different fabrics when outlining.

2 Frequently the textures will surprise you and not give you the look you think they should. It's a learning process, so don't give up.

3 Give some thought to the fabrics you choose. Keep the design clear and don't let it become mush by using too many similar textures.

4 Use different sizes of plaids and textures to keep a rug from becoming boring. Don't use just one size.

5 Use different values to keep your rug alive and interesting.

6 The more you use textures, the more you will love them.

7 Textures replicate the beauty of antique rugs and give your primitive rug a depth that is impossible with dyed, solid fabrics.

8 Use different weights and thicknesses of wools for a great primitive look.

CHAPTER FIVE

Color and Color Planning

Rug hookers refer to a wall of wool as "Eye Candy."

Because the actual technique of rug hooking is relatively simple to learn, a primitive rug's success and appeal often rests on color choices made by the rug hooker. The fabrics and colors chosen to hook a particular pattern require skill and willingness to take a chance. It is even more difficult when you decide to only use textured fabrics.

Think about how frequently you use color in your daily speech: tickled pink, feeling blue, turning green with envy, so mad you saw red, and so on. So how can you be afraid of approaching color, making choices, and using it? Color can create a mood or feeling in almost everyone. Rooms in hospitals are painted in colors to soothe. Some restaurants use paint colors to make you eat and hurry out. Color is a powerful ingredient in our daily life. It enriches our daily life—imagine a life filled only with gray!

Trial and error is fine when color planning your rug. Relax, create, and experiment. The way you put the colors together can make a nice rug or one that is strikingly gorgeous. To make a beautiful rug you need to consider color, value, and texture. A well executed color plan will make your eye dance across the rug.

VALUE, HUE, AND CHROMA

First, let's discuss a few basics of color and color theory. Frequently rug hookers make this concept very difficult. I'll try to make it as clear and simple as it should be. You should treat color as a friend, not as some scary ghoul hiding in your closet. Just know and remember these few fundamentals.

America, 30" x 39". Designed and hooked by Sally Kallin of Pine Island, Minnesota. Sally had a great collection of reds, whites, and blues, and this design was perfect for them. Sometimes, color determines what you will hook. This rug demonstrates great movement. Pattern available from Pine Island Primitives. AUBRY AMUNDSON

BASIC TECHNICAL TERMS FOR COLOR

1 *Hue,* which is the specific name of a color, such as red.

2 *Value,* which is the amount of light and dark in a specific color. Value can range from a very light tint to a very dark, saturated color. Swatches are dyed sets that may have pieces in 6 to 14 values. In the primitive world, we simply use light, medium, and dark rather than a complete range of values.

Note: *Value vs. hue.* You may think that color is most important, but in primitive rugs the value is critical. In fact, different hues can be used together if they are of the same value.

3 *Intensity or chroma* is the boldness or richness of color. The stronger the color is, the higher the chroma or intensity. Chroma is very easy for you to see with your own eyes. Don't make it complicated.

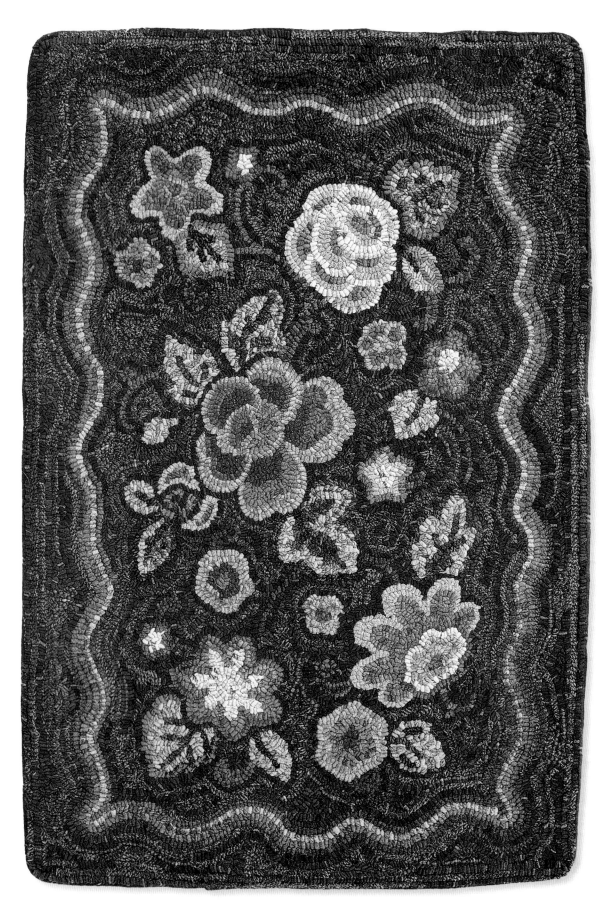

A Pocket Full, 24" x 36". Hooked by Deb Trumpour of Romeo, Michigan. Note how the colors are moved around in the entire rug. Pattern available from the designer, Kate Porter of Loopdeeloo.

Blue Cat Rug, 22 ½" x 37". Hooked by Kathleen Donovan of Watchung, New Jersey. This beautiful rug appears almost monochromatic from a distance. It uses 9 different paisleys. The colors are wonderful. Pattern available from Karen Kahle, Primitive Spirits. MARK BALA

COLOR THEORY AND COLOR PLANNING

Remember when you first started coloring? You joyfully mixed colors and you didn't hesitate in picking the color to use next. Something you found so easy as a child should not scare you as an adult.

Understanding these simple color terms will help you color plan your rug:

1. **Primary colors:** red, yellow, and blue.
2. **Secondary colors** include orange (mixture of red and yellow), purple (mixture of blue and red), and green (mixture of blue and yellow).
3. **Tertiary or intermediate colors** are combinations made by mixing primary and secondary colors. Intermediate colors are yellow-green, blue-green, yellow-orange, red-orange, blue-violet, and red-violet.
4. **Monochromatic** refers to using one color in many shades, tints, and values of that single hue. It can also include almost white and almost black. Placement of the shades creates contrast and interest.

Cottage Garden, 32" x 31". Hooked by Patti Tubbs of Beavercreek, Ohio. This rug is a wonderful example of monochromatic rug hooking. Designed by Karen Kahle; pattern available from Primitive Spirits.

When working with color, your best friend is a good color wheel. You will notice that the lightest color, yellow, is normally at the top of the wheel with the darkest color, purple, at the bottom. The other relationship that you should remember is that colors opposite each other on the color wheel are complements: yellow vs. purple, red vs. green, orange vs. blue. When dyeing, complements can be used to tone down or darken a color. A small amount of the complement will soften the original color, while a larger amount will darken the original color. And too much of the complement will turn the fabric into "mud" or a neutral.

Color wheels range from $4 to $100 and come in a wide variety of styles. First buy an inexpensive one to play with, but I bet you will soon want a better one. One of my favorites is the Artist Color Wheel because it is small, lightweight, inexpensive, easy to use, and contains a ton of information. It is not difficult to find at art supply shops and some big box hobby shops. Another favorite that's a little more expensive but fun to use is Johannes Itten's The

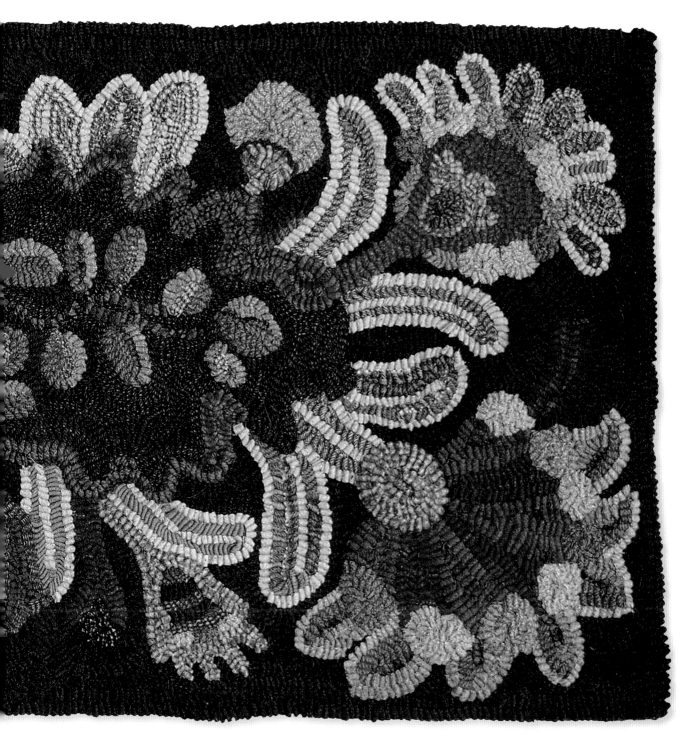

Color Star. This one also shows options with either a dark or light background. A myriad of books on color are available for you to read; but you can always just trust your eyes.

We tend to make color planning into a complicated operation when the best tools are the ones we already own—our eyes and brain. A few basic guidelines provide lots of help when color planning, but it is important to simply look and observe. You can buy a ton of books, take classes specifically on color and study for years, or you can simply observe art

Petals and Posies, 23" x 48". Hooked by Pam Fogle of Ballwin, Missouri. What an elegant and soft primitive rug this is. Note the various colors used. Pattern available from Woolley Fox.

exhibits, rugs at shows, color combinations that people wear, and nature. You should study rugs or paintings that you like and figure out why they appeal to you. Now, which sounds like more fun to you?

BASIC GUIDELINES FOR
COLOR PLANNING AND CHOOSING COLORS

Old Penn Primitive, 24" x 37". Hooked by Carol Daugherty of South Bend, Indiana. The cuts used in this beautiful rug range from #8 to 9. Because of the placement of color, your eyes flow over the rug. Pattern available from Holly Hill Designs.

1. Do not use equal amounts of light and dark. A rug that is 50% light and 50% dark will not be pleasing to your eyes or brain. It is too balanced. Unequal proportions are best. You usually don't even need to think about this because your larger percentage is usually the background.

2. Do not use equal amounts of each color. Once again, if the rug is too balanced, it won't be pleasing to the eye. One of your colors should be a little more bold, but use it sparingly. This is frequently called *poison*. A little poison is good; too much is bad in primitive rugs.

3. The only place you may want some balance is in the placement of your colors. This is not necessary, but it does make a prettier rug. Our ancestors frequently didn't balance color use, but I suspect it wasn't for lack of trying but rather because of lack of materials.

I used a variety of recycled textured fabrics in *Border to Border*. An easy way to color plan is to start with one fabric and build other pieces around it.

Border to Border, 29" x 46". Designed and hooked by the author. Build your rug from one piece of fabric.

4. In primitive rugs we prefer textured fabrics—that is fabric with a design, contrasting weave, or even bumps. Examples are plaids, tweeds, checks, herringbone, boucle. Most of us use these fabrics directly off the bolt, after washing and drying. And using over-dyed textures is fine. However, I don't use solid fabrics, whether they are over-dyed or not, or spot dyed fabrics in my rugs. To my eye, both of these stand out from the textured fabrics and thus are not pleasing. But that doesn't mean you cannot use them. Remember it is your rug; make it pleasing to your eye!

5. An easy way to color plan is to start with one fabric you like and build from it. An example is my *Border to Border* rug. I started with the plaid that has green, blue, beige, and red in it. This fabric was from a Pendleton pleated skirt, so I had plenty of yardage. The color plan grew from that one piece of fabric. All the fabrics were recycled.

6. Another easy plan is to pick a fabric with a multitude of colors and use that fabric as your guide. Then choose differing amounts of each color from that piece of fabric.

7. Some rug hookers first decide on their background value and color before selecting colors for their design. Most beginning rug hookers find this technique easiest. It works especially well if you know the specific place you will use the rug.

8. When all else fails, have a teacher color plan your rug or let her help you. But don't expect this to be a free service. You are drawing on many years of knowledge and experience of the teacher. Some teachers will work with your wools and walk you through the steps. This is great as it gives you a hands-on learning experience. Others will tell you what to use and where to place it.

Miss Lillies, 20" x 30". Hooked by Deb Trumpour of Romeo, Michigan. The turquoise is poison in this rug and is used more than usual, but it works because it is balanced. Designed by Janice Spaulding.

9. When you have all your possible fabrics gathered, it's time to trust your eye. Pile the fabric loosely on a table or floor in an area you will pass several times a day. If a fabric jumps out, take it off the pile. Yes, that is part of color planning.
10. Add some poison, those wools that are a bit shocking in color. Use them carefully so they don't overwhelm the rug.

But the true test to correct color planning is to trust your eyes. Trust your judgment. Make it simple. Look at nature. Look at people's attire. Remember, this is your rug—make something that pleases you! As an example, compare the next two photos of *Star and Fans*. Both are beautiful and they basically use the same color families, but they are quite different. One uses a higher chroma than the other.

Antique Coverlet, designed by Old Tattered Flag. Hooked by Crystal Brown.

Star and Fans, 16" x 30". Hooked by Janie Featherston of Tyler, Texas. The colors are bright and clear in this rug, thus it has a higher chroma than the other. Pattern available from Pine Island Primitives.

Star and Fans, 20" x 40". Hooked by Sylvia Hale of Humble, Texas. The beauty of this rug is that it has color, but the color is muted and softer. Pattern available from Pine Island Primitives.

CHAPTER SIX

The Power of Backgrounds

Berks County Bouquet, 17" x 21". Hooked by Grace Hostetter of Claysville, Pennsylvania. Note how the dark background makes the design come forward. Pattern available from Woolley Fox.

REIMAGINED RUG   **Berks County Bouquet,** 20" x 22". Hooked by the author. The light background softens the design. I took off the numbers and added a primitive star in place of one of the hearts. Texans love their stars! Pattern available from Woolley Fox.

T he empty space your design rests on is simply called the background. But there is nothing simple about this space. It can turn your rug from boring and bland to stupendous and exciting. It can transform your rug into a warm, comfortable, antique-looking piece or into a modern work of art. Yes, the background is that powerful!

When designing and hooking a primitive rug, the background can make your rug a joy—or a job—to hook and view. Now you know why this will be one of the longest chapters in this book. The background is that important!

LIGHT? MEDIUM? DARK?

Rug hookers in general seem to have much more trouble with background choices than with the main design of a pattern. The struggle includes not only what color or value to use, but also how to hook the background. Each decision has many variables, and that is why rugs look different even if the same pattern is used by several rug hookers.

The easiest way to think this through is to first decide if you want a light, dark, or medium background. At this stage, you don't even need to think about color—only think about value—light, medium, or dark. A light value creates a softer and often

Paisley Hearts, 30" x 24". Designed and hooked by the author. The gray background made up of 14 different recycled fabrics immediately tones down the bright reds and oranges. Use your imagination to visualize how the rug would look with a dark or light background. The result would be very different.

Newburyport, 44" x 30", designed by Edyth O'Neill, Woolley Fox Designs. Hooked by Cynthia Norwood, 2015.

This rug incorporates many points discussed in this book. The motif is outlined with several different purples and it is filled with many fabrics of a similar color and value. The borders are hit-and-miss. A myriad of fabrics were used in the "clouds." The blue sky is hooked with 8 different fabrics in a random, zigzag hooking technique. Several widths of wool were used, some left over from previous projects. Note the purple break line between the border and the clouds and the orange beauty line between the clouds and the sky. A large plaid was used for the simple border.

warmer result. A dark value makes the design jump forward and become more dominant, resulting in a dramatic rug. A medium value tends to age the rug and make it look more antique. The darker value is normally the easiest to work with, while the medium value is the most difficult. But if you want to age your primitive rug instantly, medium value is the one you want—it creates a rug that is soft, subtle, and warm to the eye. It takes a little more forethought and planning to use a medium value. You need to make sure that all the edges of your design will be either a light or dark value and that none will be of the same medium value; otherwise, the design will be lost.

If some of your design elements blend or fade into your background, simply add a few loops of a fabric that can be seen but isn't too shocking. This is called shadow hooking. You use a narrower strip and don't pull the loops as high as those around it. Several examples of shadow hooking can be seen in *Kris Kringle* on page 87. I use purple for this effect; I never use black, although some rug hookers do. The contrast of value should not be too extreme or you will draw the eye only to that line of hooking and not to the entire rug. Or if you like the antique look, do nothing: frequently in old rugs some or all of the design fades away in the background.

COLOR COMES AFTER VALUE
Once you have decided on value, start thinking about color. The most common colors and easiest to use are antique black, browns, dark blues, beiges, and tans. The most difficult color to use is gray—

and especially medium value gray. Gray tends to draw color from the design and make the rug appear to be cold or dead. If you want to use gray, I suggest giving it a wash of color or using it with a design that is vibrant. But just because the neutrals listed above are easier to use doesn't mean you should ignore other colors. In fact, one of my own favorite rugs has a green background, and I have seen some luscious rugs with red backgrounds.

Choosing which color to use is much easier than most rug hookers make it. If you are still in the color planning stage, simply layer the fabric you plan to use on top of various possible backgrounds. Place them on a table or the floor for a few hours or several days. You will be amazed how quickly you will decide which one you like the most. If this doesn't happen, then just remove the ones you like the least. Leave the others alone for some time until you make a final choice. If your design is already completely hooked, place one background option at a time near several spots of the design. Repeat with each fabric. You will most likely be pleased how quickly you decide which fabric or combination of fabrics appeals to you the most.

Because I personally find hooking the background to be boring and time consuming, I pick my background value and color when color planning the design. This way, while I am hooking the design, I can also hook one row of background around the design or maybe fill in a complete area. This accomplishes two things: it gives me instant feedback that the background fabric works and it decreases the amount of background left to hook after the design is completed.

The most difficult color to use is gray—and especially medium value gray. Gray tends to draw color from the design and make the rug appear to be cold or dead. If you want to use gray, I suggest giving it a wash of color or using it with a design that is vibrant.

HOW MANY FABRICS TO USE IN THE BACKGROUND?

You can choose the safe route and use only one fabric in your background as in *Band Box Squirrel*. This works well because the design is relatively busy and a multitude of background fabrics would compete with the design. But even one fabric can work well in a simple design, as shown in *Antique Pinwheel*.

You can be adventuresome in your background and make medium dark and dark values of two different colors work very well together. Those colors create an interesting background but don't detract from the design in *Eagle*. My personal preference is to use as many fabrics as I can when hooking the background. In this manner, it leaves little chance that I will get bored or run out of wool. And I know I will like the finished look. The highest number of fabrics I've used is fifteen and that was in a small wall hanging. *Paisley Hearts* on page 58 used fourteen different fabrics for the background. So don't let the size of the pattern restrict the number of fabrics you use. In the small piece, the colors were similar but not exact, but most importantly the values were very similar. So have fun with the background choices you make.

Above: Band Box Squirrel, 21" x 32". Hooked by Debbie Regan of McMurray, Pennsylvania. Only one fabric was used for the background in this busy design. The pattern was designed by Edyth O'Neill and can be purchased from Woolley Fox.

Opposite page, top: Antique Pinwheel, 27" x 32". Designed and hooked by the author. The medium value background tones down the brighter orange paisleys and the purples used for outlining. The idea for this rug was based on an antique rug.

Opposite page, bottom: Eagle, 26" x 37". Hooked by Barbara Knight of Humble, Texas. Note the great way the dark and medium values were used in the background. Pattern designed by Edyth O'Neill; available from Woolley Fox.

Barn Floor Floral, 25" x 38". Hooked by Jane Dunaway of Brandon, Mississippi. Values of brown are hooked in single lines around the design. Pattern available from P is for Primitive.

Opposite page: Texas Trio, 27" x 52". Hooked by Crystal Brown of Washington, Pennsylvania. The background echoes the design but uses groups of lines rather than single lines. Pattern available from Woolley Fox.

HOOKING STYLES FOR BACKGROUNDS

There are so many different ways to hook the background. If you read my first book, *Creating an Antique Look in Hand Hooked Rugs*, you are familiar with most options available. You can check that source for additional photos of great rugs. My preference is to only hook one row of background around the design as I go and not to think at all about what else I will do with the rest of the background. That thought is floating in my brain, however! I let the rug's design tell me what will look the best. I just let go and don't think about the background. By the time I have finished hooking the design, I just know what to do. But in case you want more direction, here are a few options.

Echoing is the easiest method of hooking the background. It is a technique that comes to us from the quilting world. The rug hooker simply follows the lines from the design. There will be small random areas to fill where the echo lines do not meet. *Barn Floor Floral* echoes in single lines using a couple of closely related values of brown. This carries the movement of the flowers to the edge of the rug. *Texas Trio* echoes a little differently by using not single rows, but rather several rows of the same fabric at a time. The use of single rows with differing values would compete too much with the more complicated design of *Texas Trio*. Both of these rugs are excellent examples of how to echo in your background.

Blocking is another technique that can be either subtle or distinctive. Blocking frequently is done with sharp, straight edges—like drawing squares or rectangles. But that is not necessary. *Floral Trio* is a great example of blocking without straight edges. The blocking in this rug is done with neutral colors in similar values, but varying colors and values can be used as well.

Straight line backgrounds are perfect for Orientals, but they can work for primitives as well. The fabric needs to have some variety, either in value or color, to keep it interesting to the eye, as shown in Emma Lou Lais's *Primitive Sheep*. The straight line of background hooking contrasts nicely with the curves and curls of the large sheep.

Floral Trio, 23" x 34". Hooked by Irene Shell of Woodinville, Washington. Irene used various values in irregular blocking, but it doesn't detract from the beauty of this antique design. Pattern is included in this book. See the original and samples hooked by others on pages 8 and 9.

Primitive Sheep, 29" x 32". Hooked by the author. Although one of the reds used in the background was very bright, it works because it was used minimally and with only a few loops at a time. Designed by Emma Lou Lais; pattern available from Emma Lou's Primitives.

Old Nutfield, 34"x 65". Hooked by Carla Fortney of Glendale, California. Her background pattern carries out the curves of the flowers and the flower pocket holders. Also note her interesting border and binding treatment. Designed by Joan Moshimer; pattern available from W. Cushing.

Two Old Deer, 22 ¹/₂" x 48". Designed and hooked by Sally Kallin of Pine Island, Minnesota. The background is more interesting because more than one technique was used. There is some echoing mixed with random hooking. Also, your eye is drawn to the border because of the mixture of fabrics used. Pattern available from Pine Island in two sizes. AUBRY AMUNDSON

C or S shapes is another interesting way to hook the background in specific areas. Simply echo the shapes of those letters until the hooking rows meet, and then fill in the small remaining spots. But Carla Fortney took this another step further in *Old Nutfield* by repeating a spiral in a lighter value within the background. I think you will agree it's a very nice result. Another option is to hook a specific design in the background first—either in the same fabric as the background or different value or even a different color. Stars and hearts are perfect to use in this manner.

Simple Gifts, 24" x 32". Hooked by Kathleen Bennett of Huffman, Texas. Pattern available from Primitive Spirits.

For Cynthia with Love, 25" x 31". Hooked by the author. Designed by Barbara Carroll of Woolley Fox.

Hit-and-miss is a method many prefer as it seems to hail back to our historical roots where the rug hooker used whatever color was left to finish a rug to put on the floor or on a bed. *Simple Gifts* by Kathleen Bennett used hit-and-miss not only in the border, but also in the entire background. Note that less color but several values were used in the center background. Thus the charming animals are not lost in the movement of the background. In *Antique Serenity*, the rug carries the hit-and-miss technique to the edge. It's a great old-looking rug with color in the center and along the border. The red centers in the clam shells provide continuity throughout the rug. In *Pocket Full of Poseys*, hit-and-miss was used in the corner triangles very effectively by repeating colors used in the design. *For Cynthia with Love* is my attempt at a hit-and-miss rug, and I am not a hit-and-miss rug hooker. My personality doesn't allow the freedom that other rug hookers seem to have with this method. The animals are hooked hit-and-miss, but with basically one color family for each. The other hit-and-miss areas were more free-flowing but gave me a headache. But I had to do it—it's always good to force oneself out of one's comfort zone and to push the limits no matter how great or small they may be. This rug is in the Magdalena style, and while these colors are bright now, in a hundred years they will be part of a neat muted antique rug. Most of the antique rugs that we love were originally hooked in much brighter colors than they appear.

Antique Serenity, 24" x 52". Hooked by Shirley Dusky of Romeo, Michigan. Pattern available from Monika Jones.

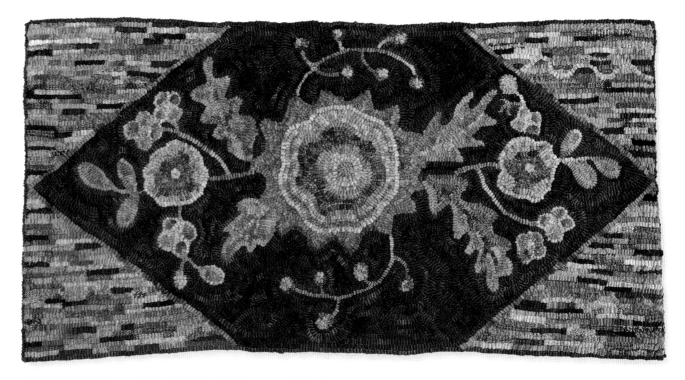

Pocket Full of Poseys, 18" x 36". Hooked by Jan Frankel of Concord Township, Ohio. Pattern available from Primitive Spirits.

Imagine how much fun you could have mixing all these neutrals in one background.

Free form is my favorite way to hook background. The style is often called willy nilly, higgly piggly, zigzag, or random hooking. Working in a small area at a time, I hook in a zigzag line by jumping up a few holes and then back down a few holes. The row of hooking is always moving forward, not backward or straight down or straight up from the previous loop. You can hook several loops in a row without creating a strict pattern. By hooking this way, you cover more area more quickly and create a randomness that works especially well if you are using several fabrics. You must be careful not to pack the loops.

In conclusion, your background should support your rug's main design—not overwhelm or overshadow it. To use a common phrase, the background should be the bridesmaid, not the bride. Study the backgrounds in rugs you like. Check out websites to study rugs. Try different methods. Notice what others are doing at camps, workshops, or exhibits.

HOOKING YOUR BACKGROUND

1. Decide on value—light, medium, or dark.
2. Choose a color.
3. Hook one row around the design.
4. Let the rug tell you how to hook the background.
5. Have fun with it.

Opposite page: Monsieur Paisley, 32" x 43". Hooked by the author using only paisleys for the motif. Designed by Barbara Carroll from a sketch of an antique paisley pattern that was never made into a paisley shawl. Pattern available from Woolley Fox.

CHAPTER SEVEN

Borders and Binding

B inding techniques for primitive rugs generally reflect the design and techniques of the rug as a whole. Primitive rug bindings often appear simple and can be very subtle. But don't be fooled. They have been created with great care to enhance the overall feeling and presentation—the essence, if you will—of a primitive rug.

The process of hooking a rug includes choosing colors for the motifs and background, deciding to have a border or not, and finally, deciding on the type of binding or finished edge. Borders are not a necessity for every rug, but you can take a mass-produced pattern and make it special and unique by adding your own border. The binding can softly finish the rug or it can add an exclamation point, depending on the technique and fabric you use.

TO HAVE A BORDER OR NOT

Many antique rugs had no border. Some had a couple of straight lines of a contrasting fabric to make a very simple border. In *Maple Sugar Hearts*, several straight lines alone make an appealing border. The same colors used in the center motif were repeated in the border.

Left: Maple Sugar Hearts, 30" x 14". Hooked by the author. Designed by Barbara Carroll. This simple design with a simple border makes an interesting piece. Pattern available from Woolley Fox.

Opposite Page: Virginia Fraktur, 41" x 24". Hooked by Debbie Regan of McMurray, Pennsylvania. Your eye is drawn quickly to the center of this rug. No real border is needed to define it. Pattern available from Woolley Fox.

Mario, 16" x 24". Hooked by author. Designed by Laurice Heath. Owned by Lauren Wade. A repeating triangle with fun colors makes an interesting border for this simple design. Pattern was available from Fredericksburg Rugs, now owned by I Love Rug Hooking.

You can also take a geometric design and repeat it for an interesting finish as in *Mario*, above. Colors not used in the design were drafted for the fun border, but some of the dog's body fabric was used to create continuity. Note the corners are calm because they use fabric from the body of the dog. Clam shells and lambs' tongues can be used the same way. But be careful that the border doesn't become the most interesting part of the rug. Its role is to support the main design.

Night Crow originally had a totally different border that didn't appeal to me—so I simply added lambs' tongues or shells along with "Welcome" at the base of the rug. The lambs' tongues were hooked in darker tones to complement the raven. Rarely do I hook dates or initials, but this rug just seemed to call for the addition. So once again, let the rug talk to you.

IDEAS AND SOURCES FOR BORDERS

So where do you find ideas for borders? Study antique rugs that you see. If you like the border, sketch it and save it. You don't need to limit your search to rugs. Quilt templates are excellent sources for borders or corners. But you can even open your eyes further! On a trip to Paris, I was amazed by the many patterns in the grates and iron work on balconies. A ton of photos are waiting for me to design another rug. More recently while in China, antique roof tiles gave me ideas for future projects. But you need not travel to foreign sites to find interesting patterns, just open your eyes. Other free sources include the design series books from Dover. Frequently rug hooking books will offer free designs for your personal use. If you love only the border, feel free to use it. You need not use the entire design of a free pattern. But do give the designer credit.

Night Crow, 18" x 23". Hooked by the author. Designed by Ramona Orihill for PRIMCO Patterns; available through Honey Bee Hive Designs. The dark border with bits of color keeps it interesting but doesn't detract from the proud crow.

Sterling, 32″ round. Hooked by Kathy Applegate, Fort Worth, Texas. Don't you love all the action in the squirrel's tail? Although very simple, the binding complements the design and doesn't take your eye away from the squirrel. Pattern available from Woolley Fox.

Front edge of Sterling

Sterling's binding was completed by Betty Grimes, of Fort Worth, Texas. Kathy is a fabulous and prolific rug hooker, but she doesn't like to finish her rugs. Luckily she has found someone who does a good job on that step. Don't let your rugs remain rolled up in the corner. If you don't like to do the binding, find someone else who will do it for you.

For all patterns, pay close attention to copyright restrictions.

The binding is frequently considered a border on primitive rugs. Think of the binding as the finishing touch to your rug. I doubt you would get dressed for a special event and forget to finish your hair and makeup. The binding is the piece of jewelry that makes the outfit perfect. Some binding techniques look best on specific rugs. In *Garden Gone Wild*, Diane used antique paisley in the hooked section, and she took it one step further and used a gorgeous paisley piece as the binding.

Detail of *Geometric Leaf*. Hooked by Dorothy DeLaune of Covington, Louisiana. Design based on a rug in author's collection. Strips of wool from the fabric used to hook the border were whipped around the edge of the rug to create the binding. The look is successful and made effective use of the fabric. She let the fabric create a great border and binding in this rug. See entire rug in Chapter One, page 11.

Garden Gone Wild, 13" x 43". Hooked by Diane Tutt of Tyler, Texas. The wonderful color flow makes this rug a great centerpiece. The use of antique paisley in the design and as the binding just takes it one notch higher. Pattern available from Pine Island Primitives.

Lulu Circles. Designed and hooked by Sally Kallin. Sally used proddy hooking for a very effective border on her clipped rug. The height of the proddy works well with the height of the clipped loops. Hooked in #9 and 9.5 widths. Also note the luscious gold background. Pattern available from Pine Island Primitives. AUBRY AMUNDSON

SPECIAL FABRICS FOR GREAT BORDERS

Now that you have finished your design, how do you decide on a border? It's always best to repeat some of the fabrics you used in the design motif when hooking the border. The fabrics that work best and are fun to use are large plaids. If you have a plain border with no detail, this is the route I would take and the plaid doesn't have to contain colors from the motif. The plaid just shouldn't be so wild that it detracts from your center. If you have a border that has a design on it, hook the design first then pick the background fabric for the border. You might want to choose something that is darker than the interior background or you can even use the same fabric that you used in the interior background. Rarely do rug hookers use a lighter fabric on the border.

HISTORICAL WAYS TO BIND RUGS

Years ago, a rug hooker would hook the rug and simply turn under the edge of the burlap. She would then stitch the burlap down with needle and thread. Those are the rugs you can find now with torn, raveling, and worn edges. Then some rug hookers hooked through two layers of burlap at the edge of the rug, thus having nothing to turn under. Neither of these methods stood up well to wear and is not recommended for floor rugs. The next "improvement" was wrapping the edge with cotton binding. This helped the edge survive longer, but the look doesn't appeal to all primitive rug hookers. The next method was to use yarn and whip the edge of the binding. This technique performed better and it's easy to find a great range of colors to use. However, I think whipping looks best with a finer cut of rug hooking. With the primitive style, I prefer using wool fabric to bind the rug and I have used this method since the 1990s. It's easy, quick, wears well, and looks great with primitive rugs.

STEAM YOUR RUG

Regardless of the binding method you choose, your rug will need to be steamed first, before you finish the edges. I use a Eurosteam iron that works well for me. Others use professional steamers or have their work steamed by their dry cleaner. But the most cost effective way to steam is with your own iron at home. Place your rug on a thick towel or waterproof surface. Place an old wet towel on top of your hooking. Have your iron setting on high. There is no need to set the iron on steam as you will be creating your own steam. Start in the middle by placing the iron directly on the center of the wet towel. Leave it there without pressure for about 10 seconds. Continue this process until you have completed the entire rug. Some areas may need to be steamed twice if you hooked too tightly. Let the rug stay in that spot until it is dry.

In conclusion, you will find many ways to bind or finish the edge of your rug. Look at finished rugs and see which style appeals to you. Talk to other rug hookers about their finishing techniques. Most of us are willing to share, and you may gain pearls of wisdom. Read different books or magazines and observe rugs at exhibits. Soon you will find one you prefer. Whichever finishing method you choose, do not rush the job. Take your time and do it well—or hire someone who does a nice job to do it for you.

Potted Padulas, 33" x 30 ¹/₂", designed and hooked by Carol Weatherman of Mustang, Oklahoma. Pattern available at *www.thesampling.net*. CAROL WEATHERMAN

Since the motifs in the rug were so colorful, the border called for color too. The stripes draw the eye to the main motif. I especially like the neutral triangles of three sides pointing toward the center and I like that the other triangle is red. The drooping flowers contrast with the flowers standing at attention, adding more interest.

Ginger Rose, 42" x 33". Designed by Janice Johnson and hooked by Ginny Waldera, Lakewood, Colorado. Available from Wooly Woolens.

All rugs do not need a border and this is an excellent example. Note how the corners frame the center and the small rectangular blocks of different values complete the feeling of a border. I love the straight-line hooking in the background and the soft, primitive look of the rug.
CHERYL BOLLENBACK

CYNTHIA'S FAVORITE METHOD FOR BINDING PRIMITIVE HOOKED RUGS

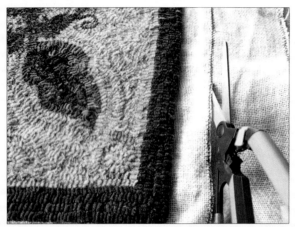

Mark dots 1¾ inches from the hooking. Connect the dots. Zigzag on that line or serge. Trim. (Steps 1, 2, 3 below)

The rolled edge of linen shows the double fold of the 1¾ inches of backing. Tack the rolled edge with a small running stitch. (Steps 4, 5)

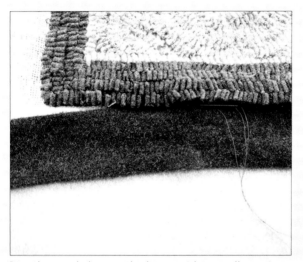

Sew the wool close to the loops with a small running stitch. (Step 7)

The wool is folded to the back and stitched with hidden stitches. (Step 8)

Wool fabric edging is wonderful for primitives. These step-by-step instructions may sound complicated, but if you take it one step at a time, it's easy.

Before I start hooking, I take a quarter and place it at each corner of the pattern and draw around the arc of the quarter as it touches both sides. This makes a very shallow rounded corner. Use this tip, and you will have no mitered corners to fuss with.

When you are finish hooking your rug, you are ready to begin the binding.

1 First, mark dots at least 1½ inches from the edge of your hooking all the way around your rug. I prefer 1¾ inches from the edge in order to get the finished width I like. Then connect the dots and round the corners. It is important that the width you marked be the same all the way around the rug so the finished edge will be the same width.

2 If you have a sewing machine, zigzag along the line you have just drawn on the backing. If you want a wider finished border, then leave up to 2 inches of excess backing. (It's not impera-

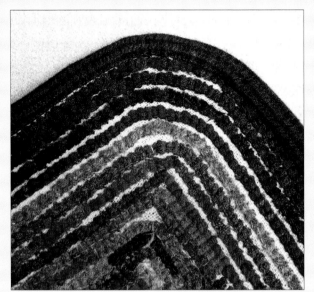

If you don't see the foundation on the back of a primitive rug, it has been packed too tightly or filled with too many loops and rows of loops. Back edge of *Worm Delight*.

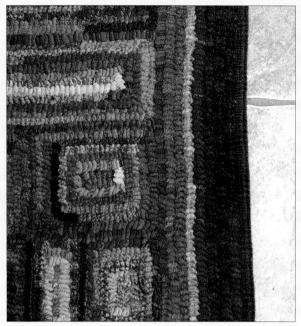

This close up of *Worm Delight* shows the finished edge.

tive to zigzag this edge. But if you don't, only trim the excess backing a few inches at a time rather than cutting it all at once. Otherwise the backing will ravel and leave a mess as you are working on it.)

3 After zigzagging, trim the excess backing.

4 Double fold the 1½ inches of backing toward the back of the rug. (i.e., fold the excess backing in half, and fold it in half again, folding toward the back of the rug). Using a basic running stitch, stitch the folded backing in place with any kind of thread. Some like to fold the material to the front, but I fold it to the back so it will be easier to stitch the fabric closer to the last row of hooking.

5 The corners will be the hardest to do. Just take it slowly, and if you have a few bumps or pleats, don't worry. Once the rug is steamed and the edge covered with fabric, it will be fine! Some rug hookers will run a gathering line around the edge of the corner. And remember, I hook shallow rounded corners, rather than a sharp point. The corners are not noticed once the primitive style rug is finished.

6 Then, steam the double-folded edge. This step sounds unnecessary, but it gives the rug a much nicer finished look and makes it easier to work with when adding the fabric binding.

7 The next step is to cut a contrasting or color-coordinated piece of wool about 2 inches wide. The wool can be cut or torn on the straight of the grain; it's not necessary to cut on the bias. Choose a wool that looks good and is tightly woven. Place the wool on top of the rug with the raw edge against last row of hooking. Place it as close as possible to the last row of hooking. Stitch the wool fabric down by hand. I use a shorter needle and take a couple of small running stitches and then a backstitch as close as I can to the edge of the wool nearest the last row of hooking. Yes, there is a raw torn edge of the wool next to the last row of hooking. Trust me: it will be perfect when finished and steamed.

8 Next, turn the wool strip of fabric to the back of the rug. Turn the raw edge under so the wool strip of fabric will be lined up perfectly on the back with your last row of hooking. Stitch the wool strip to the foundation. (You don't have to turn the raw edge under. You can just stitch it to the back of the hooked piece.)

9 Steam the bound edge. That's all there is to it.

CHAPTER EIGHT

Special Primitive Rugs

Spring Garden, 41" x 24". Designed and hooked by the author.

When you make rugs, you are creating works of art that will last more than a lifetime. Others will appreciate your work and talent for years. And when you make a special rug for a special person or occasion, you are also creating something that will be loved and appreciated.

Adding words or symbols to your primitive rug designs to commemorate weddings, births, holidays, or special events is a fabulous way to personalize a rug. And best of all, these durable, special rugs can then be passed to the next generation. These rugs can be fun or serious.

The first rug I made that I consider special is *Spring Garden*, which I designed and hooked in 1990 for the guest room my young nieces used for overnight visits. It has moved from house to house

over the past 24 years and always finds the perfect spot to land. So don't let the thought "Where will I put the rug?" hold you back. If you love it, hook it. It will always find a home—whether in your home or someone else's. Although my nieces are adults today, they always know which guest room is theirs when visiting.

If you don't create a pattern especially for your special rug, find a commercial pattern you think is appropriate. For one niece, I chose *Pear Tree* but made a few changes. In this piece, I used mostly antique paisley shawl fabric for the motifs. Another niece received *Dutch Compass and Doves*, hooked in her favorite colors. For my nephew and his wife, I used more somber colors in *Fraktur*, but I left off some of the design and added the date and initials. Needless to say, all were appreciated and placed on walls where they can be enjoyed for years.

Pear Tree, 30" x 23". Hooked by the author. Adapted from Notforgotten Farm/Lori Brechlin. Design by Spruce Ridge Studios. Owned by Lauren Wade.

Dutch Compass and Doves, 12" x 36". Hooked by the author. Designed by Bea Brock, Hill Country Rug Works. Owned by Sarah King.

Fraktur, 20" x 20". Hooked by the author. Designed by Susan Quicksall, Holly Hill Designs. Owned by Katy Smesny.

Memorial rugs, whether they are designed and hooked for personal, public, historical, or political events, are another category for rug hookers. Nada Ferris's cat memorial rug is a contemporary example of rugs that were created to pay tribute to a lost pet or family member. Frequently the antique memorial rugs would have a halo of lighter colors hooked around a deceased pet.

Kitty Rug, 27" x 39". Hooked by Nada Ferris of Hayward, California. Designed by Pat Cross. The light fabric shows how important the cats were.

Above: Wendell Eagle, 37" x 56". Hooked by Kathy Stephens of Houston, Texas. This Joan Moshimer pattern is available from W. Cushing. I love the red background and the strength of the gold scrolls surrounding the eagle.

Opposite page: Battle Flags of Texas, 50" x 24". Designed and hooked by Patricia Turner of Dallas, Texas. Memorial rugs need not pay homage only to people, pets, or holidays. This rug memorializes Texas.

Patty Turner has memorialized some of the Independence Flags of Texas. If you know anything about Texans, you know we love our state and think it's the best. This rug represents some of the state's early history. The flags include the first flag of the Republic in the lower right corner. Texans love stars now, and from this flag, you can tell the love affair started early. The Alamo flag is the 1824 flag. The flag on the left is the Gonzales Flag with the cannon and star and the posting, "Come and take it." The San Jacinto Flag is the center motif of the rug. This area was the location where Texas won its battle for independence from Mexico when 743 Texans defeated 1500 Mexican forces in 18 minutes.

You will frequently see antique rugs with eagles as the main design. Kathy Stephens's rendition is one of the best primitive interpretations I have seen. The red background is unusual and sets the gold border off beautifully. This shows that a great rug can be made by using a simple design.

> You will frequently see antique rugs with eagles as the main design. Kathy Stephens's rendition is one of the best primitive interpretations I have seen.

"Several different fabrics were used
for the fur in Santa's coat. In the best tradition of primitive rugs,
if you run out of one fabric, use something else. "

Above: Turkey and Pumpkins, 18" x 24". Hooked by the author. Designed by Laurice Heath. Pattern available from Fredericksburg Rugs, now owned by I Love Rug Hooking.

Opposite Page: Kris Kringle, 33" x 22". Hooked by the author. Designed by Barbara Carroll, Woolley Fox.

Holidays are another great excuse to hook a special rug. I know a couple of rug hookers who only hook holiday-themed rugs. The two holiday rugs I have hooked are visible year round. Just because they are holiday rugs, you don't need to hide them the rest of the year! Both rugs utilize antique paisley and wool strips ranging from #8 to 10 cuts. *Turkey and Pumpkins* is an example of a marbleized background. I used gray in the tail feathers to soften the design. The coat in *Kris Kringle* is a good example of mixing reds and oranges together. Don't be afraid to mix unusual colors. Also note that several different fabrics were used for the fur in Santa's coat. In the best tradition of primitive rugs, if you run out of one fabric, use something else!

CHAPTER NINE

Leftovers, Scraps, Worms, and Jewels

Piles of worms on *Argyle* rug pattern. Organize your strips in the way that is easiest for you—organize either by color or by value.

After you have created your first hooked piece you will notice that you accumulated a pile of leftover cut pieces. Rug hookers fondly refer to these orphaned cut strips as worms. The very small scraps are called *jewels*. And you will be amazed how quickly that stash of worms grows. Yes, there are ways to make them disappear: give a bag to a new rug hooker, donate a bag to your guild for group projects, or train yourself to cut only what you need for your current project. I find the last option is easier said than done.

I have found another fun way to empty these bags and baskets! Hook a rug using mainly worms and small leftover pieces. If your personality allows you to hook a real hit-and-miss, these pieces are perfect and ready for you to start hooking. But if your personality is more like mine, you will need some order.

HOW TO ORGANIZE

You can separate the pieces in either hues or values. I separate mine into colors or hues. Then if need be, I create a second category of values within a color family. *Argyle* was hooked completely with worms and jewels.

Colorado Cabin was the first rug I hooked while trying to deplete my worms. It was based on an antique rug and was hooked in the late 1980s using only scraps and worms from recycled fabrics from earlier rugs. The strips range from #3 to 9. When using a #3 cut along with such wide strips, I just hooked two of the narrow strips together at once and pulled them as high as the wider strips. This rug is quite at home in our mountain home in Colorado. Although it was made with leftovers and recycled wool, it's pleasing to the eye and appears as if it were carefully planned and executed.

The second leftover rug I hooked was *Worm*

Colorado Cabin, 30" x 60". Designed and hooked by the author. This rug was made using leftovers along with some recycled wool. I was determined to rid my stash of the narrow cuts from previous projects, so I hooked the narrow strips two at a time.

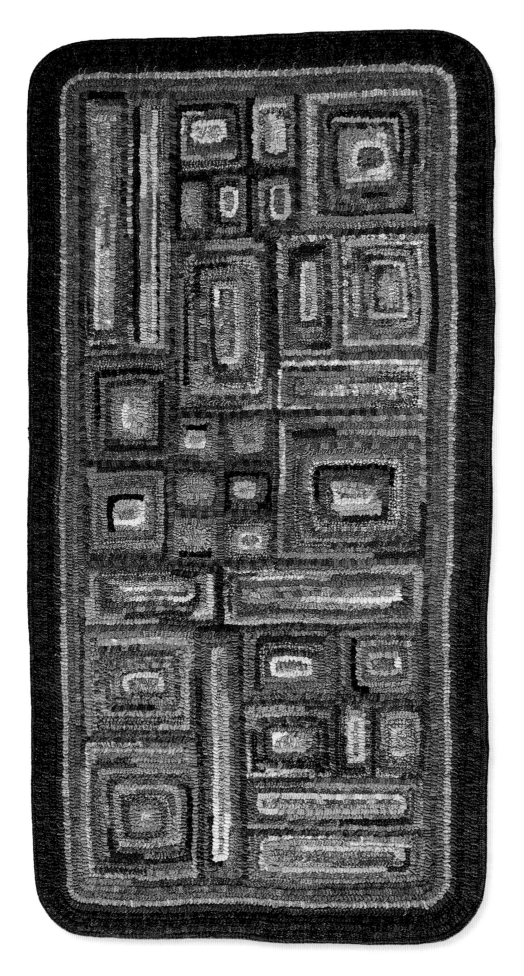

Above: Antique Cornucopia, 33" x 56". Hooked by author from an antique rug in the Bybee Collection, seen in 1995 at the Dallas Museum of Art. A limited number of this pattern is available from Cynthia Norwood, *canorw@aol.com*

Opposite Page: Worm Delight, 55" x 29". Hooked by the author. Designed by Bev Conway Designs. Except for the border and paisley centers, only leftover strips from past projects were used to create this rug.

Delight. I only used new fabric for the border, and I cut antique paisley for the center of each block. The rest of the wool was small scraps and cut strips. I started this rug with a real color plan about 2003, but only hooked a couple of blocks. The rug wasn't speaking to me, so I put it away. Yes, sometimes that happens even to teachers and people who have hooked for years.

But as my pile of leftovers increased again, I remembered the stashed-away rug. In 2012, I located it, pulled out the already hooked section, and started over. Now, it is one of my favorite rugs. It is simple but shows some continuity because I used an antique orange paisley in the centers of the blocks or squares and the fabric from a Pendleton skirt in the break lines between the blocks. The cuts ranged from #8 to 10.

The leftover piles and scrap bags were now smaller, but they were definitely not gone. In *Antique*

Cornucopia, the background and some of the border were newly cut, but the rest of the wool was all from scraps and worms, which become jewels when turned into a rug. If you look closely you can see the range of colors and values used in each area. What a fun rug it was to create.

But still more worms were around, and they were composed of a little of this and a little of that. I separated them into color families and used them in *Argyle.* The main design was organized with specific colors for each of the diamonds but with a range of values in each, while the background and the border were more of a hit-and-miss.

So don't think of those worms, scraps, and leftovers as something to hassle with or hide away. Think of them as jewels for future projects. As part of my décor, I store my worms in separate baskets in my hooking room.

Argyle, 23" x 44". Hooked by the author, 2014. Pattern available from Woolley Fox in Keeping the Past Alive series.

How Does Your Garden Grow, 37" x 21". Hooked by Thirza Youker of Fort Wayne, Indiana. Designer unknown. Original rug is owned by the author. Thirza used the original design as the jumping off point and ran with it to create her own rug. Many different fabrics, pieces, and strips from previous projects were successfully used in the rug.

CHAPTER TEN

Tone Down Your Wool

Compare the bright plaid original with its toned down version.

Today rug hookers have fabulous ready-to-use wools. But sometimes you want your wool to look different from the original piece and, consequently, different from that of other rug hookers. Even if you are too fearful to approach chemicals and dye pots, you still have several easy ways to change your wool. Primitive rugs do not normally use high chroma colors. So if you have beautiful high chroma wool, you can easily make it perfect for primitive rugs with a few simple tricks.

There is one step that some people skip. But I think it is important whether you are dyeing with chemical dyes, natural dyes, or experimenting with recycled fabrics. Always presoak your wool; it's not necessary to wash your wool first.

There are two methods and both begin with warm water.

- Soak the wool overnight (beginning with warm water) with a few drops of hand dishwashing detergent (any brand).
- For quicker results, use a few drops of Jet Dry for dishwashers or Synthrapol from PRO Chem. The wetting agents in Synthrapol and Jet Dry will make your wool ready in a few minutes.

Presoaking the wool breaks down any chemical barriers remaining from the manufacturing process and removes any residue on the surface of the fabric. And presoaking allows the dye to easier penetrate the wool. If the dye does not penetrate, you may have an undyed strip of color appear when the wool is cut.

The color was removed from a piece of fabric and that liquid, often referred to as the "blood," was used to dye a piece of off-white fabric. Green is the original wool; gold is the result of color removal. The blue is the result of using the blood on off-white fabric.

DYEING WITHOUT USING DYES

Removing Color

If you have a wool that is a little too bright for your color plan, don't toss it aside. Remove some of the color and make it more muted by simply putting a presoaked piece in a large pot with a small amount of Johnson's baby shampoo. Simmer the wool for about 15 minutes and some color should be showing in the water. Do not boil the wool as the heated water will ruin your wool by felting it or changing its texture.

Now you have to make a decision—do you like how it looks now? If yes, remove it from the pot. Place it in a clean pot with fresh water and $\frac{1}{3}$ cup of vinegar. Let it simmer for about 30 minutes. Or you can leave it in the original pot and simply add vinegar directly to the water. Let it simmer for about 30 minutes; the piece of wool will soak up most of the color from the water. The piece of wool will have the same colors, but they will be more muted or in different locations.

You can do this same process using Arm and Hammer baking soda. Use about 1 teaspoon to begin. You can add more, but don't add too much as it can also change the feel, or hand, of the fabric. Note: make sure you use a large pot as there will be a chemical reaction that will produce bubbles when you add vinegar.

Another way to remove color doesn't even require using the stove. Place hot water in your sink, and add Arm and Hammer washing powder or Tide (without bleach). Mix well, then add your piece of fabric and wait for 20 minutes. It takes longer to remove color this way, and it doesn't work with all fabrics. You may need to repeat the process. Drain the water, add more hot water, and wait 20 more minutes. Once you have a shade you like, remove the fabric and place it in a pan of water with vinegar. Put the pan in the oven for about 1 hour at 300 degrees.

After you are finished, test your wool for colorfastness. One easy way is to wet a narrow strip, place it between two white paper towels, and steam press it. Open the paper towels and check if any color remains on the paper. If only a tiny amount of color remains, your fabric is safe to use; if there is a lot of color, you need to repeat the heat and vinegar process.

Using the Blood to Dye

When you remove color this way, the water with the dye in it is often referred to as "blood." This blood can be saved and used to overdye light fabrics or vivid colors. It is also perfect to use if you have a great plaid that has a white line in it. The blood will tone down the white line and make that piece of wool easier to use. Simply add the presoaked wool to the simmering blood. Cover and simmer for 20 to 30 minutes. Add about $\frac{1}{3}$ cup vinegar (you don't have to add a specific amount, just enough so the color is helped into the wool). Simmer until the water clears. To figure out what color blood to use, pick up your color wheel. Choose the color's complement to tone it down. So to tone down a red, use a green wash; to tone down a purple wool, use yellow. Rarely can you

Browns—originals on top and married result underneath. Most fabrics will bleed, some more than others. I have discovered that browns are the most likely to not bleed.

- Don't rush—take your time.
- Never boil wool.
- Don't worry about details.
- Practice safety around steam and heat.
- Don't use the same containers for dyeing as you use for food preparation.
- Have fun and experiment.

Into a large pot of simmering water add 1 teaspoon baking soda. Add the blue background fabric. Now add other pieces of fabrics—they can be any color or any value and any size. If you stay closer to blue tones, the process will be shorter. If you want to make the fabrics darker, add some black fabric. Simmer the wool, uncovered, for 30 minutes, stirring randomly. You may be surprised at the color that appears. Just because it's blue fabric, that doesn't mean blue will seep out—it could be red or purple or even green. Eventually, all that colored blood will go back into all the wool.

Now you add vinegar, which will push the color back into the wool. The more wool you have in the pot, the more vinegar you will need. Start with ⅓ cup. Make sure you are using a large pot because the chemical reaction between the vinegar and the baking soda will create lots of bubbles. Simmer until the water clears.

You can use this process for large batches of wool or for smaller pieces. Be careful around heat and steam. Both can cause burns. Experiment and have fun.

Antique black is a background that many primitive rug hookers love to use. But it is not only black: antique black usually contains purples, browns, blues, reds, and greens. It still performs as a solid dark mahogany from the distance, but up close all the beauty is visible. It is a background that will definitely hold your interest; it is mellow rather than harsh, which is what you might get with off-the-bolt fabric. Dark backgrounds are popular because they make your design pop and, consequently, your rug is more dramatic. So don't be afraid to mix a number of different colors when marrying fabrics for a background. This process is a great way to make a variety of small, unrelated pieces of fabric work together.

get blood to dye dark values. This technique is mainly used for light or medium values.

If you have a solid black fabric you are considering for a background, please don't use it as is. First remove some of the color, and then reintroduce the color with vinegar. This will soften the original color and make it more beautiful. It only takes a few minutes and it will make a better rug. Experiment with different pieces of fabrics to see what color the blood will be. Black fabric doesn't guarantee you will have black blood! You can also have fun bleeding plaids. So live a little, have fun, and experiment!

Marrying Wools

This process is normally used for backgrounds. It's easy and works great. Suppose you want a medium dark blue background but you don't have enough of one fabric. Here's what you do.

Onion skins, walnut hulls, and avocado pits can be used to naturally dye fabrics.

USING NATURAL PRODUCTS TO DYE

I love to use a few natural dye products that also happen to be great for beginners to use. When using onion skins, wet your wool and soak it in vinegar. Place the wet fabric in layers in a flat pan. Place a layer of fabric and a layer of onion skins, then sprinkle lightly with non-iodized salt. Add another layer of fabric, onion skins, and salt. Repeat several times. You can use the same color fabric or different colors. If you use several different colored fabrics, some color will bleed into the other fabrics. Place the darkest colors on the bottom. Add a small amount of water—just enough to keep the wool from burning and sticking to the pan. Cover with tented foil and bake 30 minutes at 300 degrees. Cool and rinse. To get beige, use purple or red onion skins. For a more golden look, use yellow skins.

Another method is to simmer the onion skins and make a dye bath. Strain onion skins out to obtain the blood. You can put this blood directly onto pieces of wet fabric in a pot of simmering water. Start with a small amount and add more as desired. Simmer 10 minutes. Add ¼ cup of vinegar and simmer 20 more minutes. Rinse well. Leftover onion blood can be put into ice cube trays and frozen for later use.

Use black walnut hulls to "age" your wool. The hulls can be placed directly on pieces of wool and baked or simmered on the stovetop. Or you can simmer the hulls for hours to make a stronger dye bath. Make sure you use an old pot as the hulls will stain. Use vinegar to help the wool accept the walnut bath.

Avocado pits will give you a great flesh color. The problem is you will need several of them, so plan on making a large batch of guacamole! Simmer the pits in water until you see color. Add the fabric, simmer 10 minutes, and add vinegar. Simmer another 10 minutes. For darker spots on the fabric, place the pits directly on top of the fabric; do not stir.

Experimenting with Recycled Wool

The easiest, safest, and cheapest way to begin your dyeing career is by removing color from recycled clothing. Experiment with both solid and textured fabrics. Tear off a small piece of fabric (or use a waistband or a scrap of fabric you would never use to hook) and place it in a pan of simmering water. Add 1 teaspoon baby shampoo or 1 teaspoon baking soda and watch what happens. Within minutes, color should begin to bleed from the fabric. Add a different piece to the pot. You will discover that this process is so much fun. Remember to add vinegar to help the color set.

For information on gathering and processing recycled wool, check out my first book, *Creating Antique Hand Hooked Rugs*.

FINAL NOTES

Do not shock your wool by taking it from hot water directly to cold water. Rinse it with water that is gradually cooling or simply set it aside and let it cool naturally before rinsing. If your wool is still bleeding color after you rinse it, return it to a vinegar/water solution and simmer or bake it longer. When processing large amounts, I will allow my wool to cool gradually and then place similarly colored wools in the washer for the rinse cycle. I dry wool in my dryer on the permanent press cycle. (Clean the dryer filter after each load—you don't want a house fire!) It's best to dry extra thick wools on a clothesline.

CHAPTER ELEVEN

Patterns, Designs, and Copyright

Navajo, 30" x 31". Hooked by Crystal Brown. Golds and blues make this an interesting rug, but the simple border keeps your eye on the main design. Pattern available from Woolley Fox.

Primitive rug designs abound in today's world. The sources are endless, prevalent, and right at our fingertips. When you start to design your own primitive rugs and begin looking for ideas and inspiration, you'll be pleasantly surprised and creatively inspired!

SOURCES, IDEAS, AND ADAPTATIONS

Today is a great time to be a rug hooker, especially if you think you can't draw. We are lucky to have a large number of great designers for primitive and antique-looking rugs. One designer even has a specific section of antique patterns called "Keeping the Past Alive." All you need to do is subscribe to

ATHA (Association of Traditional Hooking Artists) or *Rug Hooking* magazine to peruse the ads from designers. Take the time to check out their websites or order their catalogs to find the perfect pattern for your next project. Or attend rug camps and notice what is available in the camp store. Make sure you don't miss viewing the exhibit. It's the perfect place to take note of patterns or designers that appeal to you.

However, just because you buy a preprinted commercial pattern doesn't mean you need to follow every line. Those lines are just guides; they are not drawn in stone. Be flexible with them. A very simple way to change and make the pattern more personal is to remove something or add something.

Bowl of Flowers, 18" x 28". Hooked by the author. Designed by Ramona Orihill for PRIMCO Patterns. I changed the border of this rug completely and used leftover background fabric strips for the binding. Pattern available through Honey Bee Hive Designs.

It is quite legal and proper for you to make changes to a commercial pattern. In fact, I highly encourage this action. You should make a design more personal and leave your own imprint on it. The design still belongs to the designer and that design is copyrighted. But you can add "adapted by (your name)" on the label you create for the rug. I loved the central design in *Bowl of Flowers*, but the border didn't appeal to me at all, so I changed it. Don't be afraid to take chances and make changes to patterns you purchase.

But you will get the most satisfaction from designing and hooking your own pattern. Start with something simple, add a border, and have fun! A great source for simple and fun designs can be right at home—your children or grandchildren. Early patterns were influenced by samplers, quilts, and coverlets as well as art. Common items in the rug

STRAIGHT OF GRAIN

A pattern must be drawn on the straight of grain to give you the best results. If you buy a preprinted commercial pattern, make sure it is printed on the straight of the grain. If it isn't, I suggest you return it.

To find the straight of the grain, place a pencil in one of the holes and drag it to the opposite edge. That gives you a straight line. Draw a line in both directions on your backing.

Here is the test: To check if a commercial pattern is on the straight, place the pencil in a hole on the outer border line. Drag it to the edge of the pattern. If it is drawn on the straight, your pencil should follow the printed line. Repeat in other directions to check for straightness.

Hannah's Barnyard, 30" x 51". Hooked by the author and created from templates provided by Barbara Carroll and Jule Marie Smith.

hooker's life such as pets, houses, and local scenery made good subjects. Study old rugs, quilts, wallpaper, fabrics, and paintings for ideas or inspiration. But don't copy from catalogs. These drawings are copyrighted—more on that subject later. There are sources you can directly copy—some Dover books, some websites, and some instructional books—which give printed permission to copy. You can also make paper templates of animals, shapes, or flowers and place them directly on your backing to outline.

HOW TO TRANSFER YOUR DESIGN

You can transfer your pattern several ways, but this method is the easiest I have found. You will need a pencil, a permanent marker, and Pellon interfacing, which can be purchased at a fabric store and through some rug suppliers. I like to use a thin Pellon with small red dots or blue lines. These markings are useful to keep your pattern straight, and the thinner Pellon allows your ink to penetrate easier.

First of all, you need the drawing. You can draw your pattern to scale, or you can simply take a smaller original drawing to a copy shop and ask them to enlarge it to a specific size.

Now you place the Pellon over your paper design and weight it down. Trace it with the pencil. Then place the Pellon tracing over your linen foundation. With a new permanent marker, SLOWLY trace the pencil lines on the Pellon. The ink from the marker will penetrate the Pellon and leave design lines on your linen. If the ink does not saturate the Pellon, you need to trace slower. You can retrace the design directly on the linen when you remove the Pellon if the lines are not dark enough. Your Pellon tracing can be reused.

Make sure you leave 5 inches of foundation around all edges of the pattern so that it is easy to put your pattern on your frame and to complete the binding process.

If you design your own rug, keep in mind the Golden Rectangle that furniture makers use in order to achieve the perfect size for a rug that will be appealing to your brain. This is the formula: The length should be 1.6 times the width. So if the width is 30 inches, make the length 48 inches.

UNDERSTANDING COPYRIGHT

Copyrights are an important part of discussing rug hooking patterns. What is copyright? It's a law to protect the artist and the artist's work. That means you cannot "copy" another person's work legally. If you copy someone's work you are at risk of legal action—the least of which would be a cease and desist order and the worst could be a lawsuit. Basically, for rug hooking, any work published before 1923 is in the public domain. But if you see a line drawing of an antique rug in a recent catalog, you can't take it to a copy store and make copies. Although it is an antique rug, the line drawing is copyrighted. That business has invested time, energy, talent, and money creating that specific line drawing. It belongs to them and is protected. If you copy it, you are stealing their work. A great website with more information is *www.copyright.gov.*

Rug hookers have a keen eye and frequently see greeting cards they like and would like to hook. Once again, that card is copyrighted. But all is not lost. Check out the information on the back. Contact the

Mimi's Belle Epoque, 29" x 47". Hooked by Crystal Brown of Washington, Pennsylvania. Note the various repetitions of circles throughout this rug. Gorgeous! Pattern available from Woolley Fox.

company. Let them know in a written format what you would like to do. Surprisingly, most of the time permission will be granted and they may request a photo of your finished work. Just make sure you keep a copy of the correspondence for yourself and another copy with the rug.

It is unethical for one member of a group to order a pattern then trace it and give copies to her friends. That is copyright infringement and stealing from the original artist. One pattern was paid for and that should not be copied. Teachers are aware of this, and if they suspect a pattern has been copied, they will not work with it. Many teachers are also designers.

If you see an antique rug that you love, simply sketch it. Take measurements and notes and make your own pattern. Or even better, take a photo of the antique rug and later make your own pattern from your own photo. Do not make a pattern from a copyrighted photo in a book.

Some rug hookers think if they change the design it is now theirs. Not true! You can make changes to a design, but if it still reminds us of the original, it's considered copyright infringement. So why take the chance? The best thing to do is either completely design your own work or buy patterns from designers.

Don't let copyright scare you. Just think it through and I'm sure you will make the ethical, legal decision.

Distelfink, 22" x 25". Hooked by Grace Hostetter of Claysville, Pennsylvania. The colors in this piece are high chroma and very dramatic. The dark background makes it even more dramatic. Pattern available from Woolley Fox.

CHAPTER TWELVE

Final Thoughts

I want you to enjoy hooking your rugs, so here are a few thoughts I would like to leave with you.

1 You are making your rug, so hook the pattern you want in the colors and manner you prefer. Friends or teachers can help you, but don't let their comments box you in. This piece of art has a long life and will be a remembrance of you to others.

2 Don't be afraid to make changes in commercial patterns. Those lines on the design are not drawn in stone; they can easily be changed or ignored. Leave your personal imprint on a commercial pattern so it will be different from others who hook the same pattern. Don't we all want to be individuals?

3 Try designing your own pattern. It's easier than it sounds—just open your eyes to the patterns and colors around you. Visit rug exhibits and museums. And don't forget about closer-to-home sources, like children's or grandchildren's drawings.

4 Color planning is easy; don't over-think and make it more difficult than it need be. You already have the best tools for color planning—your brain and your eyes. Gather the colors you are interested in using and pile them in a spot you will pass several times a day. You will quickly see which fabrics should be removed or used in a limited way. Remember that color choices are very personal.

5 In primitive rugs, be sure to use more than one fabric in a motif or design. You can even be bolder and use several fabrics when outlining the motif. Keep those fabrics close in value.

6 Use many fabrics in your background. In a dark blue background, for instance, pieces of purples, dark reds, browns, and even almost-black fabrics will be much more interesting and more fun to hook. If you are using an interesting plaid, only that one plaid may create the same result.

7 For variety and interest, use different widths of wool. Most of us have a favorite width, but add movement to your rug by using other widths. I love to mix in hand-cut strips. Remember: many rugs were created without the use of cutters. This is a great way to use leftover strips of wool from previous projects.

8 For a more primitive look, mix the weights or thicknesses of wool. Use some wools that are lighter weight than you usually use. We all love the way the more densely woven wool feels and hooks, but take a chance and use some of the thinner wools. You may need to fill a few more holes than normal, and you may love the result.

9 Value your creation and your creativity. When someone says "Great rug!" simply say, "Thank you." Don't make excuses, like "My teacher told me what to do," or don't belittle the rug or say, "It's nothing." It is something! We hook rugs as an extension of ourselves; we love to take something flat and colorless and turn it into a work of art. While for many it is the process we love, the result is an item of beauty others will enjoy. Take the time to enter your work in a contest, fair, or exhibit to share your work with others.

10 Most importantly, have fun no matter what style you hook!

The patterns here can be enlarged to whatever size you like. All of these rugs appear in the book. The sizes given are the sizes from the original rugs.

Roses with Leaf Scroll, 25" x 44"

Spring, 29" x 42" or 24" x 35"

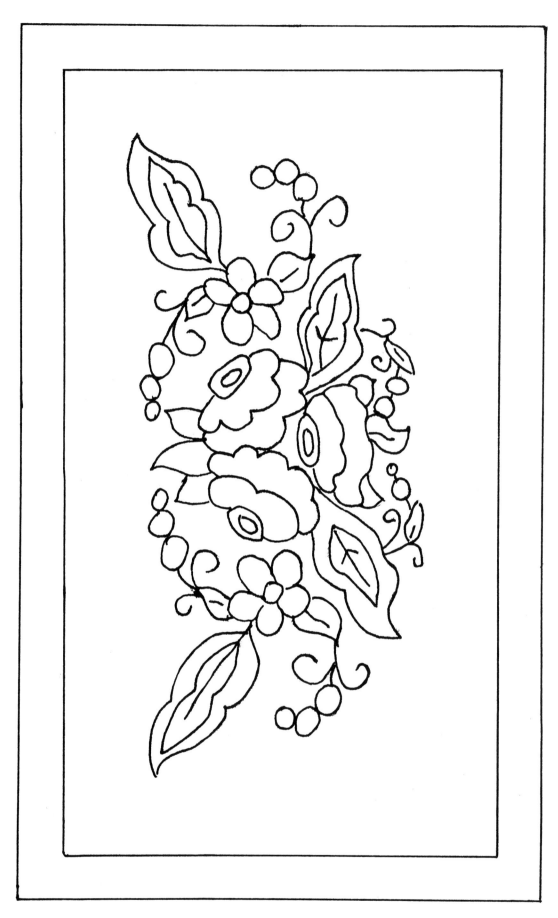

Floral Trio, 21" x 34"

Three Grand Roses, 26" x 44"

Flowers and Scrolls, 24" x 36"

Simply Eight, 25" x 37"

Trio of Circles, 15" x 44"